D1599089

The English Parish
600-1300

CHURCH HISTORY OUTLINES
EDITED BY V. H. H. GREEN, D.D.

The English Parish
600-1300

JOHN GODFREY

Published for the Church Historical Society

LONDON S·P·C·K 1969

First published in 1969
by S.P.C.K.
Holy Trinity Church
Marylebone Road
London N.W.1

Made and printed in Great Britain by
The Talbot Press (S.P.C.K.)
Saffron Walden, Essex

SBN 281 02334 4

Contents

Foreword

This series of Church History Outlines has been designed to keep the reader in touch with the findings of recent scholarship without having recourse to the apparatus of the learned study. The books will consist either of revisions of topics of major interest based on the collation of the works of modern scholars or of more specialized studies founded on original research and illuminating themes which have significantly affected the history of the Church.

This book falls into the first of these categories. The parochial system has come under fire in recent years, as, for instance, in the Paul and Morley Reports, so much so that thought has been, and is being, given to its modification and reconstruction. The geographical area of the parish, its inequity in terms of population and finance, the curious system of patronage which seems somewhat haphazardly to provide the parish with its parson, suggest to many that the parish as it is at present constituted is an archaic survival from the past. Contrariwise many feel that the parochial system is so much part and parcel of the Church of England that its radical modification, and certainly its complete disappearance, could only mean spiritual impoverishment. It is not for the historian to decide whether it is archaic or not, but he must be interested in the way in which it came into being.

He cannot dispute that it is very much a survival from the past. Its origins are lost in the mists of early church history. The history of its development is fraught with difficulty, for it is a mosaic of scattered fragments, enshrined in the findings of learned journals and books. Mr Godfrey, himself a parish priest, has skilfully woven the threads into a tapestry and has made what may seem a remote subject a matter of topical as well as of antiquarian interest.

V. H. H. GREEN

Preface

The main aim of this essay is to outline the origins of the English parochial organization, a subject which it is to be hoped will one day receive full and detailed investigation by scholars in this country. The parochial system has many critics today; one wishes that it had more students. And whereas it would appear that the real threat at present is not to the parochial "system" itself, but to the pastoral office enshrined within it, I have concluded the booklet with a notice of William of Pagula, a parochial incumbent in the diocese of Salisbury, who did much to familiarize the Church in England with the concept of the "cure of souls". The bibliography includes a selection of books and articles which I have found useful.

Donhead St Andrew Rectory   JOHN GODFREY

1. Continental Origins of the Parochial System

It is perhaps true to say that today the main strength of the Church in most European countries lies in the countryside. Town churches may sometimes give an immediate impression of livelier activity, but usually the broad impact which they make on their respective districts is relatively small. The country church, on the other hand, in many areas remains important socially. In England it is often regarded almost by instinct as the symbol of the Christian tradition. The disappearance or suppression of the rural parishes would undoubtedly be the cause of a great deal of regret if not dismay.

So much may well be granted. Yet it must be admitted that historic Christianity is not in origin a rural faith at all but primarily urban. The New Testament indicates the emergence of believers' circles in the towns of the Roman Empire, in seaports and commercial centres, wherever there might be a lively social scene and a constant interchange of ideas. The Church remained predominantly urban for a considerable time after the preaching of the apostles and their earliest successors. Such indeed is what one might expect of an age such as that of the Antonines, when the Empire was a vast concourse of cities, rivalling each other in the pleasures offered to their inhabitants—as the orator Aelius Aristides put it. The social and commercial life of the Empire in its golden period was concentrated mainly in the urban areas. In the ruins of the old port of Ostia, not far from Rome, one may yet see the mosaic floor, decorated around the theme of the life-giving chalice, of a room in the house of a prosperous Christian. It

1

was in such town houses as this that most of the early congregations were accustomed to meet. But from the third century there was a decline in the old urban prosperity. The villas, or country estates, became of increasing importance. As recent studies emphasize, there were large gains for Christianity in the rural areas of North Africa, Egypt, and elsewhere. During the famous Long Peace of the Church in the latter part of the third century (between the persecutions of Decius and Diocletian), the number of believers greatly increased. Buildings designed specifically for Christian worship were now probably first erected in the Empire. The idea that all churches in the Christian age of innocence, prior to the toleration of Milan (313), were "house" churches is common but fallacious. And then with the failure of Diocletian and his imperial colleagues to extirpate Christianity, and the conversion of Constantine, membership of the Church became eminently respectable, and the christianization of the Empire proceeded at a growing pace. This inevitably entailed a "fanning-out" of ecclesiastical organization, and the founding of churches in the more outlying areas.

The idea of a solitary devotee is not native to the Christian religion, which from its inception was congregational. It is on the local gathering or "family" of believers that the conception of a parochial system is ultimately based. At least as early as the opening years of the fourth century some local communities were acquiring a "parochial" air. In Syria, priests were being set over small town and village churches. The Church of Alexandria, one of the most thriving and enlightened in the whole Christian community, was notable for the degree of independence and responsibility which it allowed to its district priests. It was the church of the Baucalis locality, by the wharves and warehouses of one of Alexandria's harbours, of which the arch-heretic Arius had oversight. In his struggles with orthodoxy, it is interesting to observe, he was able to count on the backing and loyalty of his flock. In Rome at the same time there were about forty congregations, each centred on a district of the city. Throughout the Christian world, from Britain to Mesopotamia, the faithful were assembling together for the celebration of the Eucharist, and it was natural for each "family" to be the centre of Christian activity in its surrounding area. No theory or doctrine lay behind this development. Nothing else could really have happened. Men and women of like beliefs and interests instinctively gather together.

The basic unit of church organization was the *parochia,* a pre-Constantinian term of Greek origin. The word *paroikia,* in its biblical and ecclesiastical usage, implied a dwelling or sojourning in a strange land, and it was probably used first of Jewish colonies in the eastern cities, later of colonies or congregations of Christians. The word occurs in 1 Pet. 1. 17, where the reader is bidden to pass the time of his "sojourning" (*paroikia*) in fear. The New English Bible here quite misses the point. The *paroikia* or *parochia* came to denote the bishop's sphere of authority, which was centred at first on the house-community which was the commonest, though not the only, type of church before toleration; afterwards on the basilica, as a rule in a town or city. The *parochia* was presided over by the bishop, who had around him his *familia* of priests and deacons to assist in pastoral and administrative work. There would be many humbler men too, in the *familia,* in lesser orders, in effect fulfilling the duties of caretakers and domestic servants. In the case of large and important churches, in great cities of the Graeco-Roman world, the principal community would have one or two daughter communities, each with a priest, but these would be directly responsible to the bishop. The ideal was that the bishop should baptize and say mass in such churches when possible, and the pastoral cure belonged essentially to him. In Rome itself the Pope was for long the sole celebrant at the Eucharist, in different churches by turn, perhaps well into the fourth century.

In connection with the bishop's authority, we must of course consider the word "diocese". It was derived from the secular nomenclature of the Roman Empire. Under the Diocletianic reforms of the later part of the third century the Empire was divided into twelve dioceses, each beneath the vicar of the praetorian prefect. It was a division subordinate to the prefecture, of which there were four in all. In the Church's organization as it was to develop by the time of Gregory the Great (*c*. 600), the diocese was to become really an extension of the bishop's *parochia*, and the term would be held to apply particularly to the wide rural areas which by then had come to be comparatively well supplied with churches and chapels. The whole geographical area within the bishop's spiritual authority, however, continued for centuries to be called his *parochia*, while the diocese came to be regarded as the same area considered as a unit of administration.

Before tracing the development of the English parochial system, it is essential first to examine the subject briefly with reference to the two great continental lands to which the infant English Church was so much indebted. Italy is the most useful starting-point to any study of the subject. During the pre-Nicene period, Christianity was stronger in Rome and southern Italy than further north in the peninsula, where Milan, Aquileia, and Ravenna would seem to have been the only places which certainly had bishoprics. In the urbanized south, on the other hand, there were many city *parochiae*, each presided over by its bishop. In the province of Latium alone, for instance, there were no fewer than forty-four bishoprics. This distinction between the rural north and the urban south, as expressed in the foundation of bishoprics, was to last for centuries, and throughout the Middle Ages the Churches of the Germanic countries would be characterized by large and relatively few dioceses, whereas in the "Latin" lands almost every city had its episcopal see. In Italy as early as *c*. 600 there were some two hundred and fifty bishoprics; in England at the close of the middle ages there were seventeen. Today, when the English traveller visits an Italian town such as Palestrina (the ancient Praeneste) and sees the modest church which stands in the centre, it appears odd to him that what he is looking at is actually one of Italy's old cathedrals. To the native Italian it is perfectly natural.

One result of the rapid spread of the Faith following the conversion of Constantine and the subsequent State establishment of Christianity by the emperor Theodosius (late in the fourth century), was that the countryfolk became Christian on a wider scale. By the fifth century rural parishes under their rectors seem to have been emerging. By *c.* 600 such churches were a recognized and distinctive part of Italian ecclesiastical organization. These arrangements corresponded in some degree to the old imperial organization—the bishoprics to the territorial *civitates,* the parishes to the *pagi* or rural districts within them. It should, however, be borne in mind that, though for the sake of convenience we may henceforth often refer to local units as "parishes", in Italy and largely elsewhere the term *parochia* continued for centuries to come to denote primarily the bishop's sphere of spiritual authority, though by 600 it was beginning to be used also separately for country districts. To Italians of the fifth and sixth centuries these rural churches were the "baptismal" churches, from their possession of the font, which gave them, as it were, the status of self-sufficiency.

There was a further development. As the Christian mission kept up the momentum of its advance, churches were established in the more outlying country areas, though in a position of close subordination to the baptisteries. Such churches, or *oratoria,* would normally be the result of missionary work on the part of the baptisteries. And in addition the owners of the *villae,* or private estates, began to put up places of worship on their own land. The Popes were quick to recognize the potentialities of such moves, and Gelasius I (492–6) ordained that a landowner founding a private church must forgo any claim to its financial income. The project was not to go forward without papal approval in the first instance, and the church with its property should be vested in the bishop. The founder and his heirs, however, might nominate the priest who was to serve the church, a concession which was probably an acknowledgement of a long-standing custom. In the course of the sixth century such private oratories greatly multiplied, and Gregory I sought to curtail their independence by forbidding them the possession not only of fonts but of their own settled priests. The private churches were in no way to be allowed to undermine the position of the baptisteries, which were central to their neighbourhoods. The baptisteries were the "public parishes", distinct from private ecclesiastical enterprises. The crucial possession for a church was a font; a church able to offer the facilities of baptism was a "parish" church. Baptisms, it must be remembered, were still solemn and public occasions, and not the private family affairs they later became and for the most part remain.

We may now sum up the ecclesiastical organization prevailing generally in Italy during the period, *c.* 568 to 774, when the Lombards were politically in control. The system was headed by the cathedral, a city-church, and in most cases the only church within the city walls to have baptismal rights. There were some exceptions to this rule, as in Verona, a city with four baptisteries, but normally in the cathedral city there was only one church with full ecclesiastical privileges. Other churches, if any, in the city would be subject to the cathedral, the bishop saying mass in each of them by turns. Outside the city, in the countryside around it, were the baptisteries, all within the bishop's authority and often of episcopal foundation. The baptistery was administered by a staff of clergy headed by the archpriest or rector. The baptismal church was therefore a collegiate institution, and might be known as a *monasterium* and its clergy as *monachi* (without necessarily being "regulars" living under rule). The rector was in some cases chosen by the parishioners, but was himself responsible to the bishop as his superior, attending the latter's annual synod and receiving his authority ultimately from him. In the management of church property and endowments, however, the rector held an independent position.

Around the baptistery were the "oratories", serving small or scattered villages. Some of these were the result of missionary or expansionist activities on the baptistery's part. Each of them, though of course consecrated for divine worship by the bishop himself, would come within the authority of the baptistery, whose rector was expected to visit it on its annual feast. It seems that the oratories were generally served by a "pool" of clergy, mostly drawn from the lesser clerks of the baptistery. A comparatively large oratory might well have such a cleric resident on it, but others would be dependent on occasional visits.

In addition to the oratories subject to the baptisteries, however, were the proprietary churches, founded by landowners on their own soil. It is wrong to assume that a landowner was always a private person, a sort of Dark Age "squire". The owner would often be a monastery, or the bishop, or some other ecclesiastic. The owner appointed a priest to look after his church on his behalf, he himself controlling the revenues. From the owner's viewpoint this was an advance on Gelasius I, who had tried to prevent private founders of churches from being in a position to benefit materially from their pious initiative. It could scarcely have been realized at the time that these proprietary churches held the key to the future of direct pastoral administration in the West. By the closing years of the Lombard period they were widespread in all parts of Italy. They were pieces of personal property and could be inherited or transferred virtually at will. The priest was a servant of the owner, a necessary adjunct to the altar, saying mass for the same basic reason which impelled the landowner's ploughman to attend to his soil and his kitchener to cook his food. Meanwhile, however, throughout the eighth century in Italy the baptismal churches remained the central element in the ecclesiastical fabric generally.

We turn to the other continental land with which the English Church in its infancy had close and fruitful contact. Of Dark Age happenings in Gaul we have a famous if sometimes hair-raising account in the *History of the Franks* by Gregory of Tours. Gregory became bishop of the Loire city in 573, and

was a man well acquainted with secular and ecclesiastical
affairs. The picture he presents is one of a brutal and turbulent society, as the new kingdoms of the West arise from the
ruins of the old Empire. We see men turning to the Church,
as to a "haven where they would be". Christian communities
are taking root in town and country. In Gregory's own diocese
of Tours the pioneer was St Martin, who became bishop in
372. In many neighbouring villages, such as Candes and
Amboise, he built churches, after destroying the pagan
shrines and baptizing the inhabitants. It was in Candes that
he died; his shrine is now marked there by a fine Romanesque
church. Martin's successor in the see was Brice, who also
built new churches in a number of villages, including Chinon
—a place to become celebrated in French medieval history.
The country parishes (Gregory specifically writes of *parochiae*
as belonging to episcopal churches) steadily multiplied in the
course of the fifth and sixth centuries, and during Gregory's
episcopate there were about thirty in his diocese. The growth
of the country parish was probably however a gradual process. Missionary priests would not at first venture far from the
domus ecclesiae in which the bishop kept his household, and
they would be expected to return to the city church each
Saturday to assist in the Sunday services. It was as rural
Christians became more numerous that clergy were detached
from the staff of the city church and deputed to serve country
churches. They were now sent out not merely "ad prae-
dicandum" but "ad regendum". Still on the official list of the
episcopal *familia*, they continued to receive their allowances
from the common fund. But in course of time they became
settled in their respective districts as parish priests. Meanwhile,
the bishop tried to perambulate his diocese, travelling by horse
or in a wagon. The great prelate Caesarius of Arles regarded
this as a very important part of his work, aiming at visiting
each of his parishes two or three times a year.

   The advance of Christianity at this time entailed also a
consolidation of the Church's position in the cities, and we
recognize cathedral churches in the 'medieval" sense. Such

was the cathedral of Vaison-la-Romaine, near Avignon, which survives today as a parish church. It still retains in the apse the bishop's marble seat. Gregory of Tours tells us that Agricola, Bishop of Chalon-sur-Saône in the later years of the sixth century, enriched with marbles and mosaics an arcaded cathedral church which he had recently erected.

Earlier in the sixth century the growth of country churches was sufficiently vigorous to require canonical legislation to regulate it and place it within an orderly and official system. This is proof of the reality of the spread of Christianity to the rural and outlying areas. A notable series of councils was held, as at Agde (506), Clermont (535), and particularly Orleans at various dates between 511 and 541, which attempted to provide law for the rural churches now assuming importance in the Church's life.

The scheme which emerges from this legislation is one of churches ordered in three classes, approximating broadly to that prevailing contemporaneously also in Italy. In the city were the cathedral and subordinate churches, in the countryside the "public parishes" with their staffs of clerics, and on the estates the oratories or chapels. Over the city churches the bishop had direct and personal oversight. In Tours itself were three churches, served by the bishop in turn. On important festivals only one of the churches would be used, all the clergy and faithful gathering as one body for what must have been crowded and somewhat noisy occasions. It was several centuries before such urban churches secured individual parochial status.

Outside the city, in the *vici* or large villages, were public churches each served by what might be called a resident "college" of clergy—priests, deacons, and sundry clerks— under the leadership of an archpriest. They varied in size, some so large as to include young boys in training for the clerical order, some perhaps so small as to need the services of only one or two clergy. These country churches were self-sufficient entities, in that the faithful could obtain therein all

the means of grace. Here the Word was preached, mass celebrated, and baptism publicly administered in the solemn yet
joyful ceremonies of Easter Eve. The whole area around the
country church was the *parochia,* a term recognized in this
connection by the synod of Agde in 506, and would as often
as not include within it several small villages and hamlets.
The clergy were responsible to the bishop, a visit from whom
would be necessary at least for the consecration of a church
fabric. Each Lent the clergy would be required to send one
of their number to the cathedral city to obtain the holy oil
essential for the approaching Easter Eve baptisms. The bishop
both visited the public parishes on formal occasions such as
visitations and summoned their clergy to synods in the city.
The clergy of the public parishes were on the official list of
the diocese, and in theory an extension of the bishop's
familia.

Whereas the central rural churches in Italy are known as
baptisteries, those of Gaul we more frequently refer to as
minsters, a term derived from the Latin *monasterium.* The
real meaning of *monasterium* is commonly misunderstood, and
the sharp modern distinction between "monks" and "seculars"
often read back mistakenly into the conditions prevailing in
the fifth and sixth centuries. The *monasterium* at this time
was properly the enclosure within which an ecclesiastical
familia dwelt, whether the *familia* was one of clerks serving a
population or one living under a rule and probably with-
drawn from the world. In practice, the two types of community did not differ much. They dressed alike, lived
similarly in common, and recited the same office. The
"ascetics" sometimes took an active part in missionary work,
at least in areas like northern Gaul where the Faith was
comparatively new. Conversely, the title of abbot, or *abbas,*
might refer to the head of a *familia* of clerks as well of monks
or ascetics. Moreover, it was easy for ascetics or clerks to
migrate from one type of community to the other. There was
no really clear line between clerks and monks until the time of

Gregory the Great, and even after then the terms *monasterium* and *abbas* could still be used in a secular sense.

Of an entirely different order was the priest of the oratory on a *villa* or private rural estate, who had no official standing in the diocese, if indeed he was regarded as being in the "diocese" at all, and owed his appointment to the landowner and was subject to his whims and fancies. Some of the *villa* oratories had been founded by bishops on their estates, not necessarily within the bounds of their dioceses; most were the work of private lay owners. Not all of the oratories had their priests, but were dependent on sporadic and occasional visits of clergy from the nearby *monasterium* or public parish. According to the 506 Agde council, though mass might be said in a private oratory on any normal Sunday, the worshippers must on great festivals attend the public "parochial" church or the cathedral. And later in the century there was similar legislation, such as the placing of restrictions on the keeping of saints' relics in *villa* oratories. But the presumption is that if a landowner went so far as to build his own place of worship on his estate, he would normally wish to have a priest attached to it, and might select some relatively intelligent and pious servant and send him to the bishop for ordination. The priest would remain his servant, dependent on him for a livelihood. And as the idea of the purely local church, serving the needs of a village or estate, took root, in course of time there would arise a desire for such a church to get some sort of parochial status, with its regularly settled and recognized parish priest. By the middle of the sixth century, the *villa* clergy were important enough for canonical attempts to be made to bring them within the orbit of diocesan discipline. The oratory on a private estate is now beginning to be known as a *parochia*. In some cases it appears to have possessed endowments. An idea of the relative growth of minster and private churches can be obtained from the diocese of Auxerre. By *c.* 500 there was a total of twenty churches, eight in *vici* and twelve in *villae*. A century later the total number had grown to thirty-seven, thirteen in *vici* and twenty-four in *villae.* As Professor Henry Beck remarks, this is just what one might expect, as saturation point for the establishment of new minsters would be reached more quickly than in the case of oratories.

Thus the Church's ministrations became particularized in remote places, and as this happened, the tendency was for the public parishes to lose something of their old importance. By the start of the eighth century the proprietary or private churches were an established and traditional feature of the Frankish ecclesiastical system. The tendency too of the relationship between lord and parish priest was in the direction of feudalism: the priest was the lord's "man", receiving his church "saving his lord's service".

2. English Minsters

It was from Lombardic Italy and Merovingian Gaul whence came the Roman missionaries who were to leave so strong a mark on the English Church. The Anglo-Saxons also owed a great deal to the Celts from Ireland, and much ink has been spilt and many passions aroused in the past in the attempt to determine who played the greater part in the establishment of the Church in England. Amongst the Celtic Christians the primary unit was the "ascetic" monastery, which also served as the Christian centre for a district. Bishops were relatively unimportant, being in large measure functionaries for ordaining and consecrating. The Irish, who in their homeland had never known the rule of the Roman Empire, were unfamiliar with the idea of the diocese. It would not be true, however, to say that they did not know the *parochia*, which is native to the Christian religion as such. In Ireland there existed monastic *parochiae*. The Celtic abbot had a sphere of authority, a *parochia*, over his monks and over the secular folk who leaned on them for the sacraments. In England, the mission from Iona built churches, probably mainly on royal estates, for the people, and these served *parochiae*. But they were essentially offshoots of the monastic institute, and not parishes in the sense which we are to consider. Amongst the Celts a pastoral ministry always tended to be personal rather than territorial.

Bede in his *Ecclesiastical History* praises the Celtic clergy who served beneath Colman of Lindisfarne and his predecessors prior to the Whitby conference of 663. These men have no need for fine and costly buildings, he writes. They are content with a church in which to worship, and with cows as their only worldly possession. They are always on the move, preaching the Word of God. The people love them, gathering in somebody's house when a priest arrives in a village, to hear from him the message of life. The only concern of the Celtic priests and clerks is to preach, baptize, visit the sick, and care for souls. In wealth they have no interest at all. The stamp which these men left upon the nascent pastoral tradition of England must have been considerable.

It is a testimony to the part played in the conversion of the Anglo-Saxon kingdoms by Celtic missionaries that even after the arrival of Augustine in 597, for much of the seventh century, the diocesan bishop was of less significance in the English Church than he was on the Continent. We may take Theodore of Tarsus, Archbishop of Canterbury (669–90), to be the virtual founder of the diocesan system in this country. And even then the diocese was not, as in Gaul and Italy, normally the city with its surrounding countryside, but the kingdom or its subdivision. It was because of this initial difference that in medieval England the dioceses came to be few and of great territorial extent. The idea was early fixed in men's minds in this country of the bishop as a magnate, rich and splendid, ruling over a vast area in princely style, rather than as a pastor in more or less direct relations with his people. The essentially tribal character of the Church's approach to the English during the Conversion period is well illustrated by the turn of events in the midlands. The west midland region now comprising the counties of Worcestershire and Gloucester-shire was inhabited by a folk known as the Hwicce (their name survives in the Wyche Cutting which passes through the Malvern Hills). Archbishop Theodore assigned to them their own diocese, that of Worcester. Further west were the Magonsaetan, whose settlement represented the limit of the Anglo-Saxon advance into former Celtic territories. They became the bishop of Hereford's flock. The Middle Angles were in due course to secure their diocese of Leicester. It is the essentially "royal" character of the English conversion, with Germanic kings adopting the Faith on behalf of their people, which accounts for the large English dioceses. In all this it is tempting to see a continuation of the Germanic pagan idea of the king as *heilerfüllt,* standing between the tribe and the tribal gods and sacrificing on his people's behalf. In the English kingdoms it is the same story time and time again; Ethelbert of Kent, first Edwin, then Oswald, of Northumbria, Sigbert of East Anglia—the king transfers his allegiance from Woden to Christ, and the people follow. Paulinus baptizes his converts in King Edwin's presence. Edwin transforms his pagan temple at Yeavering into a Christian church. Aidan on his preaching journeys is personally accompanied by Oswald as interpreter. The frequency of the prefix "Os-", which may signify "divine", in the names of the Northumbrian kings, is worthy of remark; and there is the striking fact that the majority of Anglo-Saxon saints are members of royal houses.

In view of the particularly high honour in which bishops were held in the Anglo-Saxon Church, it is perhaps surprising that the Old English word for cathedral, *bisceopstol,* is little used. The head church of the diocese is normally classed with the minsters, though of course a very important one. The study of the bishop's *familia* is peculiarly interesting, however, and not only for its own sake but because the episcopal *familia* was the prototype of the *familiae* of the minsters generally.

The Canterbury *familia* (which has been studied with some degree of thoroughness) began with the arrival of Augustine at the head of forty monks, who were granted a house of residence in Canterbury by Ethelbert. Augustine himself had earlier received his training as a cleric in the *familia* of Felix, bishop of Messina, afterwards becoming prior of Gregory's monastery of St Andrew on the Caelian hill in Rome. At the start of the Canterbury mission he and his brethren formed a distinctly monastic community, of whom only Augustine himself and one or two others were in priestly orders. But as the mission prospered, a fresh situation arose, in which the bishop found himself presented with pastoral duties and in need of the help of men not pledged to the cloistered life. Some of his monks Augustine must certainly have now raised to the presbyterate. But he also approached the problem by establishing two churches in Canterbury. He rededicated an old Romano-British church to the "Holy Saviour Jesus Christ our God and Lord", to serve as the abode of himself and his successors. Secondly, King Ethelbert built for him a monastery, to St Peter and St Paul—though Augustine did not himself live to see its completion. It was the first of these two churches, the famous Christ Church, which became the home of the archbishop's *familia;* the second came in time to be known as St Augustine's, a Benedictine house pure and simple.

It has been a matter of dispute amongst scholars as to how far the Christ Church *familia* remained monastic or became secular. There is a dearth of charters, unfortunately, for the crucial period from 597 to the opening of the ninth century. It would, however, seem likely that Augustine's *familia* lived communally, since all the members of the original band were monks. But almost from the first, Pope Gregory envisaged the likelihood of some junior clerks of the *familia* being married men with stipends. And in later years, with the passing of the monks through death or other causes, the community would tend to become increasingly secular in character. By the opening years of the ninth century the priests of the *familia* had their own homes and were in receipt of stipends. In 813 Archbishop Wulfred tried to enforce the common life currently being advocated by ardent church reformers. He conceded to his *familia* the use of their houses, but with the observation that they should be more grateful to God for his benefits, and diligently attend the canonical Hours and make use of the communal dormitory and refectory. Wulfred's charter is attested by the *familia,* which included eight priests and several other clerks. Elsewhere in Kent there was also the bishopric of Rochester, which, it has been shown, was probably served by a secular *familia* from the very beginning.

Another Anglo-Saxon episcopal *familia* which has received close attention is that of the ancient diocese of Worcester. A

series of charters connected with this church gives us a sight
of the *familia* as it was from *c.* 800 onwards—priests, deacons,
clerks. They appear as a body of clergy who with the bishop
hold jointly the estates of the church. The members of the
familia attest the charters as witnesses, and it is evident that
the bishop makes grants of property only with their approval.
We first see the Worcester *familia* in a group of charters of
the time of Bishop Denebert (798–822). It appears to have
been regarded partly as a training school for clergy destined
to hold responsible office in the Church. In one of his very
first charters, Denebert is careful to say that he makes the
grant with the consent of his *familia*; it is not he alone who
makes it, but "the whole congregation of the church of
Worcester" with him.

From the attestations of Worcester charters which run from
the start of Bishop Denebert's episcopate for a century or more,
we deduce a *familia* of normally about a dozen clerks, perhaps half of them in priest's orders. They appear to have been
headed by a *praepositus* or provost. We see the same names
reappearing, then falling out, and new ones taking their place.

The vast extent of the English dioceses necessarily entailed
a special importance and responsibility for the country
churches, or "public parishes", within them. In England the
type of church known as a baptistery in Italy was usually
referred to as a *monasterium,* or in its old English form as a
"mynster", though it must be remembered that the term
monasterium was also used, and for centuries afterwards, on
occasion, of almost any kind of church except perhaps the
very smallest. The minster's most usual founder at first was
a king or bishop. There was no precise rule as to the sort of
clergy meant to staff it; these might be either secular clerks
or monks living under rule. Old English documents sometimes
refer to monastic or minster bodies which in fact were
"secular" rather than "religious", and one must be constantly
on guard against the tendency to draw too clear a line between
the two types of community. The head of the community
might be called *abbas* or *praepositus.* As on the Continent,

and as with episcopal households in England, the community or *familia* includes an inner circle of priests and some clerks of inferior status. Such clergy would tend to reproduce in miniature the organization and mode of life of the cathedral *familia* in which many of them had received their training. The priests say mass and all assist in singing the Divine Office. An important adjunct to the more important type of minster is the school whose primary purpose is the preparation of youths for holy orders; and secular administration of one kind or another, including estate management, will engage some members of the *familia*. Others will sally out from time to time to the villages of the surrounding countryside to preach and say mass, missionaries to a people slowly groping its way to the mysteries of the Faith.

We have two very interesting and well known instances of such perambulations. Cuthbert, who entered the Celtic monastery of Melrose in 651, was accustomed as prior of the community to go out on extensive preaching and baptizing tours through the valleys, calling on remote villages, winning the confidence of all who heard him. Sometimes he made these expeditions by horse, but more often he went on foot in apostolic manner. Such evangelistic journeys were no fad of his own, Bede specifically stating that Boisil, Cuthbert's predecessor in the office of prior, had done the same. In a valuable passage the Jarrow historian says that "it was the custom at that time amongst the English people, when a clerk or priest came into a village, for all to gather together at his command to hear the word". But though following what must have been a general practice in making such tours, Cuthbert made a special point of visiting isolated villages in rough and inhospitable country. His tours seem normally to have lasted a few days at a time, so engrossed was he in calling rustic folk to the Faith, and in persuading them to abandon the use of amulets and other forms of idolatrous superstition. His journeys on behalf of the gospel bear a resemblance to those of Aidan a few years before, who had been an indefatigable itinerant preacher from his island monastery of Lindisfarne.

It is indeed quite possible that the *parochiae,* or spheres of pastoral influence, of the two communities would meet and overlap somewhere in the wild country of the Cheviot hills. We are told how Aidan in his journeys always went on foot when practicable; this enabled him to stop and talk to anyone he met, urging the pagan to come forward for baptism and the Christian to stand fast in his faith.

Though minsters (secular and monastic) all over the country were the centres of Christian activity in the seventh century, it is likely that the Celtic *monasteria* were more forward than their Roman counterparts in promoting such evangelistic tours. The Celt was never happier than when moving from one place to another. We read how Boniface, the great apostle of the Germans, who is usually thought (though there is no certainty of this) to have been born near Exeter *c.* 675, owed the fostering of his vocation to itinerant preachers. His biographer Willibald, writing of Boniface's childhood, observes that "when priests or clerks, travelling abroad, as is the custom in those parts, to preach to the people, came to the town and the house where his father dwelt the child would converse with them on spiritual matters . . ." Devonshire was a region where in the seventh century Saxons were still rather thin upon the ground, a lordly minority amongst a predominantly Celtic population. Boniface himself was certainly of Saxon family, as his childhood name was Winfrith, which is Germanic, and he himself years later on the Continent declared with pride that he came of a distant branch of the German race. But it is probable that the Church in these parts, though by now acknowledging Roman supremacy, was strongly influenced by the Celtic outlook and way of doing things.

The distinctively Roman, as apart from the Celtic, minster in England we may take to have been relatively stationary, as intent upon consolidating its own position and investing it with dignity as on converting and instructing the peasants of neighbouring estates. Its buildings were substantial, and the impression is one of a community settling down on a particular

spot of land and making it all its own. At about the very time
when Cuthbert was making his tours and the young Boniface
was listening with awe to travelling preachers, a certain
Mercian ealdorman Friduric, in the territory of the folk
known as Tomsaetan, gave some land at Breedon in Leicester-
shire to the monks of Medeshamstede (the later Peterborough),
to enable them found a minster with a priest to teach and
baptize. This was between 675 and 691. Nothing remains of
the original Breedon church, but that the establishment went
on to prosper is proved by a fine surviving series of eighth-
century carved friezes, with ivy-scrolls and animal, bird, and
human figures. They served perhaps to decorate the screens
enclosing the area of the church reserved for the clergy and
singers. Late seventh-century fragments at South Kyme,
Lincolnshire, look as if they might have been panels in
similar screens. The Anglo-Saxon church architects in the
seventh century were much influenced by Gaulish and Italian
styles, and the great English tradition of pilgrimage to Rome
was already under way. What would appear to have been
constructed in Breedon church was a *schola cantorum* of the
type to be seen today in the church of San Clemente in Rome.
This latter enclosure, with its brilliant Cosmatesque decora-
tion, is medieval, but was constructed out of marble salvaged
from the screen previously standing in the sixth-century
basilica on the same site—a church probably visited by such
English travellers as Wilfrid and Benedict Biscop.

    Another famous daughter church of Medeshamstede, foun-
ded at about the same time as Breedon, was Brixworth in
Northamptonshire. This church survives, one of the most
remarkable of early ecclesiastical buildings in England. The
original structure was no less than 120 feet long. What still
stands is the nave, but the original church must have been
even more imposing, the large porches on either side, now
blocked up, opening into chapels or *porticus*. Contemporary,
or nearly so, with Breedon and Brixworth, is Corbridge-on-
Tyne church, built on a royal estate. Like Brixworth it was
constructed largely of re-used Roman materials, the builders

finding the nearby ruins of the camp Corstopitum a useful quarry. Corbridge church still includes the original nave walls and west tower, with its magnificent arch.

The minster church or "cirice" would of course be the centre of a community including the various offices necessary for the clergy and their attendants, such as the living quarters and workshops, kitchens and gardens, the whole surrounded by an enclosure of some kind, such as a wall or stockade. The minster of the early Anglo-Saxon Church is the spiritual equivalent of the "tun" of the first Germanic settlers in England. Some idea of the likely contents of a minster enclosure of well-endowed type may be obtained from the ruins of the Yorkshire double monastery of Streoneshalh (the later Whitby). This was a "religious" house, with a community of men and women, but its layout and equipment were probably much the same as those of a substantial secular *monasterium*. The monastery was founded in 657, on a site promised by King Oswy in thanksgiving for victory over the heathen Penda two years before. It was ruled by the saintly Hild as abbess until her death in 680. Destroyed by the Danes in their great assault on Yorkshire during 866–7 which was to lead to the establishment of the Scandinavian kingdom of York, it was later to be restored by the Normans.

Excavation of the site has shown that the Saxon establishment covered a wide area and included a varied assortment of offices and buildings. The minster church was dedicated to St Peter and served as burying-place for the Northumbrian royal house, but the large number of liturgical objects found suggests that there may well have been one or two subsidiary churches within the enclosure. Plurality of churches is in accordance with Anglo-Saxon practice as known in religious houses elsewhere, and the generally careless layout of the Whitby establishment is also Anglo-Saxon, quite unlike the systematic design of the Benedictine abbeys of subsequent times.

Evidence of many structures was found, built of exterior stone walls about two feet thick, and (judging by the absence of

tiles and slates) with thatched roofs. There were small houses
apparently intended for a single occupant each; these were
divided into a couple of rooms, which had drainage facilities
and open-hearth fires. Water was obtained from shallow, stone-
lined wells, dug in the clay. Stone paving was found on the
site. The existence of a smithy points to the general self-
sufficiency of the *monasterium,* and we read of stables. There
was also an infirmary for the sick and a guesthouse. We may
take it that there were dwellings for the craftsmen and work-
men.

Excavation brought to light large numbers of metal fragments of ecclesiastical objects, such as hanging-bowls, of the
type which have also been found in pagan Saxon graves and
are at Whitby being used in the church's service for some
purpose hard to determine, perhaps as oil lamps, or washing
basins. Various pieces of bronze would seem to have formed
parts of shrines or of book-covers, and there are many bronze
fragments of what probably were tags for book-markers. The
love of books was from an early date a notable feature of the
Anglo-Saxon churchmen. Not the least of the services of the
minster was that it introduced the book to the Englishman.

Here and there in England it is possible to recognize the
geographical distribution of the early minsters. We know of
the centres around which revolved the ecclesiastical life of the
Canterbury diocese. Besides the church of Christ in Canterbury which was the seat of the archbishop, there were seven
minsters, each significantly situated near a road or port. At
Dover a minster of secular clergy was established by Eadbald,
son of Ethelbert I, early in his reign (616–40). From the
number of the clergy attached to it, twenty or more, it is
clear that the minster was intended as a centre of pastoral
and evangelistic ministry for the surrounding country area.
At neighbouring Folkestone a minster, primarily for nuns,
was founded by Eanswith, Eadbald's daughter. According to
a late medieval tradition recorded by the historian Thomas of
Elmham, a *monasterium* was founded at Lyminge by
Aethelburga, sister of Eadbald. She was wife of the ill-fated

Northumbrian king Edwin. Like Folkestone, Lyminge would seem to have been a double monastery. A certain royal chaplain, Romanus, endowed it with the tract of land which still bears his name, Romney Marsh. These three minsters continued to hold their importance for many generations to come. In the eighth century one charter refers to the "basilica" at Lyminge, another confirms a grant of fishing rights to the community, whilst at the end of the century reference is made to the "venerable minster" known as Lyminge. In the middle of the ninth century a single charter refers to the *familiae* at Dover, Folkestone, and Lyminge.

The prominence of the royal and female elements in these Kentish minsters will at once be noticed. It illustrates very well both the part played by the kings in the establishment of Christianity in the Anglo-Saxon kingdoms, and the high prestige enjoyed by womenfolk (a Germanic trait which had been noted long before by Tacitus). Reculver, in the Thames estuary, was given by King Egbert in 669 (according to an explicit entry in the Anglo-Saxon Chronicle) to a certain priest Bassa, to enable him inaugurate a minster in that place. The fine church survived until its demolition in 1805, described by Harold Taylor as "an act of vandalism for which there can be few parallels even in the blackest records of the nineteenth century". It was taken down by the vicar of the parish, on the urging of his mother, who did not like it. Minster-in-Sheppey and Minster-in-Thanet, both founded *c.* 670, were also royal foundations. The former house, part of the fabric of whose church still exists, was founded by Sexburga after the death of her husband Eorconbert, king of Kent. The latter house was the work of Eormenbeorg, wife of Merewalh, ruler of the west midland people, the Magonsaetan. Her daughter Mildthryth, abbess of the foundation towards the end of the seventh century, seems to have been one of the very few outstanding personalities of the early Kentish Church. Two other daughters of Eormenbeorg also became nuns, Mildgyth and Mildburg, the latter of whom was founder of Much Wenlock, Shropshire. One more Kentish minster remains to be mentioned, namely Hoo, between Rochester and Tilbury, which was a daughter of Medesham-stede. All these Kentish *monasteria* are listed in a grant of privileges to the churches of Kent by King Wihtred, at the council of Bapchild (near Sittingbourne) in the closing years of the seventh century. This grant is probably suspect, occurring in a manuscript of the thirteenth century, but it is interesting to see how the churches concerned had by tradition come to be regarded as the ancient minsters of Kent.

Such minsters correspond broadly to the baptismal or "mother" churches (*matres ecclesiae*) of the Continent. They were essentially communities of clerks, though three of them (Folkestone, Lyminge, Minster-in-Thanet) were embedded in the broader framework of a "double monastery", each serving a house of dedicated women as well as the laity of neighbouring villages and estates. Each Kentish minster would have a *parochia* for which it was responsible. They were to develop into rich communities, obvious targets for the predatory-minded, and largely came to grief in the Danish invasions which made havoc of so much of ninth-century England.

In the west country the fairly considerable number of places with names compounded with "minster" suggests that here we have towns or villages which began their history as ecclesiastical centres. In Dorset we have Beaminster, Charminster, Iwerne Minster, Yetminster, Sturminster, Lytchett Minster, and Wimborne Minster. There are Pitminster in Somerset, Warminster in Wiltshire, Axminster in Devon. Further north the same type of place-name marks Kidderminster in Worcestershire and Minsterley in Shropshire. In Essex there is Southminster, though generally such names are less common in the eastern half of England. Sometimes, as at Sturminster, the name is simply that of the local river compounded with "minster". The church, not seldom, stands significantly close to the river-bank. Minster churches for long had a virtual monopoly of baptism, and in the early years of the English Church the ceremony was often performed in the open, in running water. Bede tells us how Bishop Paulinus, while at Edwin's royal estate of Yeavering in Northumbria, preached Christ's saving message to those who gathered around him, then baptizing them in the river Bowment. It is true that he also records that Augustine, at the very outset of the Conversion, was granted the old Canterbury church of St Martin, wherein to recite the offices, celebrate mass, preach, and baptize. But it would appear that in the seventh century baptism was frequently an open-air event. Fonts did not become part of the regular equipment of English churches until much later.

Throughout the missionary period of the Anglo-Saxon Church, that is to say the seventh century and well into the eighth, the minster churches were the only significant ecclesiastical centres. The fully developed stage of pastoral care, in which local village communities were ministered to by priests on the spot, had still to be reached. Paganism remained a power, and it was necessary for the Christian religion to stay entrenched behind strong defences. The picture we see is of a new faith, increasingly confident because of royal support and in its own inner resources, but not yet sure enough of itself to come out of its strongholds. Throughout England are these communities of men (and women, a fine and heroic feature of Anglo-Saxon Christianity) in their *monasteria*, saying the offices together and from time to time sallying out to evangelize the villages and hamlets around them. On great feasts the villagers try to visit the minster for the solemn celebration of mass. They are expected to bring their children thither for baptism. There is reason to believe that just as the diocese tended to be provided for the kingdom or sub-kingdom, so a minster would often be meant to serve in the first instance as the spiritual centre of a royal vill and its estates. Later, minsters were perhaps provided for provincial districts, of the type which in later times came to be superseded by more advanced forms of Anglo-Saxon administration. We are told that *c.* 705 Offa, King of the East Saxons, granted some land to Wealdhere, Bishop of London, "in the region which is known as Haemele". There is no mention here of a

minster or other church, but the ancient district Haemele is
of the sort which was probably common in the seventh
century and afterwards. The presumption is that as the
Christian mission made progress an attempt might be made to
provide a district, where possible, with its *monasterium*. The
name of this particular district survives in Hemel Hempstead.
There is a somewhat more particular example in 736, when
the Mercian king Aethelbald granted to Cyneberht, an ealdorman and member of his *comitatus* or personal following, some
land for the foundation of an ecclesiastical institution in a
district which the charter concerned states to have been known
since days of old as Ismere, in Worcestershire. In this case
the establishment is specifically said to be a monastery
eigenklöster or private-owned monasteries of the Franks,
districts we might be in a better position to attempt tracing
the spread of *monasteria* in general. The Ismere establishment
is to be built beside the river Stour, and will possess its
meadows, woods, and fisheries.

A *monasterium* might also signify a type of church community which existed in at least the Northumbrian Church
in eighth-century England, and is known as the "family
monastery". It is an institution somewhat analogous to the
eigenklöster, or private-owned monasteries of the Franks,
though not entirely so. A private person in England would
build a church with subsidiary offices on his estate, call it a
monastery, and put in his own family, and a cleric or two who
had not made the grade elsewhere, as the community with
himself as "abbot". His estate would become relieved of
secular burdens; and the practice was obviously open to abuse.
The family monastery was an institution which, properly
fostered, might have had real potentialities. We think of the
Little Gidding family community of several centuries later.
But eighth-century England was not ripe for such experiments,
and the institution petered out. It is likely that the family
monasteries eventually settled down as private churches, with
a priest to serve the family and the estate.

In the meantime, of local parish churches in the medieval and modern sense, with their rectors and vicars, there was of course no idea, though in the seventh century we do come across the first use in England of the word "parish" for a small rural unit. This was Osingadun, referred to in the anonymous life of St Cuthbert as a *parochia* belonging to Whitby abbey. But as their spiritual focal-centre the villagers in most parts of Christianized seventh-century England would probably erect a timber or stone cross on some suitable spot, and there gather as occasion served for preaching and prayer. A certain Anglo-Saxon nun who went out to serve as a missionary in Germany, Huneberc of Heidenheim, in the *Hodoeporicon* of Willibald, states that "on the estates of the nobles and good men of the Saxon race it is a custom to have a cross, which is dedicated to our Lord and held in great reverence, erected on some prominent spot for the convenience of those who wish to pray daily before it". The reference is to eastern Wessex, that is to say Hampshire; the time is *c.* 700. Huneberc is relating how the child Willibald was desperately ill, his parents offering him to God for service in the monastic life should he be spared. They offered him "not in church but at the foot of the cross". The passage is an interesting one for the study of parochial origins in England. We infer that by *c.* 700 on many rural estates there was still no church, or at least that its sanctity in people's minds was less than that attaching to the open standing cross. In other words, if a church existed at all it was probably something comparatively recent, whereas the cross was firmly embedded in the people's affections through long usage.

The idea of the standing cross as a symbol of the dying Saviour was well known in England. Bede tells how in 634 King Oswald set up a cross in the ground before engaging his foes, near Hexham, and summoned his soldiers to kneel in prayer around it. In later years the monks of Hexham made an annual pilgrimage to the spot on St Oswald's eve, keeping vigil through the night and singing mass at dawn. Subsequently they raised a church there for the benefit of the many believers making the pilgrimage. Bede remarks that the setting-up of this cross marked the start of Christianity in Bernicia. It seems certain that in many places the sequence must have been the same—the erection of a cross followed by the establishment of a church. In the course of the eighth century native Anglo-Saxon sculptors produced a splendid series of standing crosses, particularly in the northern kingdoms, the surviving fragments of which are still strangely impressive. Some of these crosses were intended as memorials of the departed, but many at least of them must have been put up in the first place to serve as focal-centres for prayer and worship in villages where as yet there were no churches.

At the foot of the cross the visiting priest said mass, but this obviously could only be at somewhat irregular intervals, and the opportunities of the people to share in the Holy Mysteries must have been limited by such exigencies as distance, weather, and the general disturbance of a district through war or banditry. By the closing years of the seventh century it is likely that purely village churches here and there were coming into being. Archbishop Theodore, in his *Penitential*, allowed a priest to celebrate mass in the open, "should this be necessary". There is something idyllic and attractive to the modern eye in the sight of a group of Saxon men, women, and little ones, kneeling round a tall, sculptured cross on the village green. But English weather was probably then much the same as it is now, and it is known that ailments such as colds in the head were troublesome. Theodore's saving clause suggests that he thought mass should properly be celebrated beneath a roof. Even the simple and austere Cuthbert, on his pastoral tours, preferred to administer the sacraments in improvised sheds rather than under the open sky. And, if it was indeed desirable that the faithful should assist at the Holy Sacrifice each Sunday, facilities must be available on the spot, not only at some central church ten or twelve miles away. It is clear that, with the passing of the purely missionary stage and the spread of Christianity to the countryside, practical considerations would call for the foundation of village places of worship.

The village churches at first were usually of wood. The Anglo-Saxons used timber as their native material, and in a land largely covered by forest and woodland there would be no shortage of supply. We can be sure that a competent job was made of the earliest English churches, by men who really understood the craft of timber construction. In the nature of things none of these churches survive. (The famous wooden church of Greenstead in Essex, though probably pre-Conquest, is much later than the Conversion period.) We have, however, in County Durham a virtually unique instance, from the later years of the seventh century, of a stone village church. This is the little church of Escomb, perhaps the best preserved of Anglo-Saxon structures. Built of stone from the neighbouring Roman fort of Vinovia (Binchester), it has been in continuous use for Christian worship since the seventh century, except for a brief interval in the Victorian period. Its plan is quite unlike that of the more spacious minsters. It is not easy to visualize a sizeable community of clerks assembling here for Divine Office; but, with its nave leading through a tall, narrow arch into a simple chancel, it would seem just right for a priest and his server along with a congregation of about thirty worshippers. One must beware of attempting to be too meticulous in discriminating between "minster" and village "parish" churches of the seventh century. To the recently converted Anglo-Saxon a church was just a church, whether it was large or small, whether it had half-a-dozen priests or only one. The surviving church of Somerford Keynes, Gloucestershire, however, seems to indicate a purely village foundation. Its heavy megalithic doorway is clearly of a very early date. It was perhaps built by Aldhelm for the villagers on a substantial estate granted to him here in 685 for the benefit of his Malmesbury monastery.

In the earliest moves towards the foundation of village churches the encouragement given by Archbishop Theodore must not be underrated. At one time it was not unknown for students to refer to him as the father of the English parochial system. This system was such a spontaneous and gradual growth that it cannot be said to have been initiated or thought out by any one person. But Theodore was virtually the inaugurator of our diocesan organization, within whose broad outlines a more localized scheme of pastoral care would be able to develop. And in his *Penitential* he shows that he had very much in mind the possibility and even desirability of the faithful being cared for pastorally by their own village priests. He would incidentally be aware of conditions in the East, where parish churches were known, and of Justinian's law of 541 which had decreed that a man building an oratory and providing a reasonable living for a priest might present a priest to it.

When the initiative was taken, however, it was by the landowners. The provision of local churches was a private venture, dictated by the need of a landowner for a church where he and his family, his household and serfs, might hear Sunday mass. Theodore did not forbid the initiative, though in the interests of ecclesiastical propriety he found it necessary to limit it. He laid down that once a church was built its timbers were not to be used for any other purposes, such as that of firewood. If a church was later removed to another place the original site of the altar must be marked by a cross. Such churches were in fact pieces of private property, though not wholly outside the realm of episcopal jurisdiction. They were not to be used until the bishop of the diocese had first consecrated them. Bede records a couple of occasions when John of Beverley, Bishop of York 705–18, was asked to consecrate private churches. The thegns concerned were Puch and Addi. John readily complied, though it is interesting to observe that the busy bishop in each case showed no eagerness to dally behind on social or pastoral business when urgently pressed to do so. Having performed his episcopal function, all he wanted was to get back with the least possible delay to his *monasterium*.

So little is known about these early village churches that it is hazardous to generalize concerning them. It is probable, however, that the founder appointed the priest, perhaps choosing him from amongst his own household or servants and sending him to the bishop for ordination. There was no question of any pre-ordination training in such cases, though presumably a candidate would be at least partly literate. It is of course possible that in some instances a thegn might himself obtain orders and say mass in his own church, though we have no evidence of this. Egbert, Archbishop of York 734–66, insisted that before a priest officiated in a private church, the bishop's approval must first be sought.

Writing to Egbert in 734, Bede describes the state of affairs in the Northumbrian Church. He pours scorn on the family monasteries. He is concerned about the lack of spiritual provision in the smaller villages and outlying districts of the York diocese. He advises Egbert (an old pupil of his) to ordain priests for these remote places, who will preach, baptize, say mass, and teach the Creed and Lord's Prayer. He is not saying that hamlet churches should be built, with priests attached to them. But he does seem to imply that by now the larger villages had their churches. What he is in effect urging is that they should have more clergy, to enable them supply the out-of-the-way hamlets and homesteads of the dales and moors of Northumbria. Elsewhere, in one of his commentaries, Bede observes that it was the custom of his contemporaries, on entering a village or town, to visit the consecrated house of prayer, should one be there. This would seem to suggest that in his day, early in the eighth century, small local churches were in existence. But they must have been few and far between.

Private churches on the estates of thegns and great laymen were more or less outside the regular ecclesiastical scheme. As far as this kind of church was concerned, the bishop would content himself with consecrating it, ordaining its priest, and approving his general suitability for the office. But by the mid-eighth century at the latest *monasteria*, whether regular monasteries or secular minsters, were also establishing

daughter churches in the larger villages within their respective
areas or *parochiae*. The canons of the council of Cloveshoe (a
centre which has not been identified), held in 747 under
Archbishop Cuthbert's presidency, convey the impression that
the *monasteria* were officially responsible, as it were, for the
Church's pastoral and evangelistic work. Priests are to say the
canonical Hours according to the "monastic" office. They must
be loyal to their "abbots and abbesses". This was of ordinary
clergy working pastorally—teaching, baptizing, visiting—some
of whom would be subject to the double-monastery type of
minster such as those of Kent. But the really interesting
thing about the Cloveshoe council from the point of view of
parochial development is the ninth canon, by which it is the
bishop who assigns a priest to his district. And it appears that
the clergy attached to the *monasterium* or subject to it are not
merely members of an amorphous "group" working in some
kind of partnership. They are assigned to their respective
localities or districts. The clergy shall carry out their pastoral
duties "per loca et regiones laicorum, quae sibi ab episcopis
provinciae insinuata et injuncta sunt". Thus the ground was
being prepared, not only by means of the private enterprise
of the thegns and others but also through the agency of the
"official" Church, for a localized parochial system.

By the beginning of the ninth century the establishment of
private churches and daughter churches to the *monasteria* had
probably made some progress, and the mission to the Anglo-
Saxon peoples was evolving into a system of pastoral care.
This is suggested by an important council held at Chelsea in
the summer of 816 for the Canterbury province, in the
primacy of Archbishop Wulfred. It was attended not only by
all the bishops of the province but by Coenwulf, King of
Mercia, within whose territories London at this time lay.
Amongst the various acts of the council are three of particular
interest for the study of parochial origins. A ban was placed
on any further ministrations of Celtic priests in the province
—it is apparent that nomadic preachers of this sort had by
now come to be regarded more as a nuisance than a help.

With the exception of the archbishop himself, all clergy of the province, whether bishops or priests, must confine their activities to their own dioceses or parishes. Instructions are given for the procedure to be followed in the consecration of new churches, to include the sprinkling with holy water and the celebration of mass. These three acts together are a pretty clear indication that by now the Church in England had become a settled institution. After more than two centuries the age of purely missionary activities was at last over, and the movement towards the foundation of parish churches under way. Meanwhile in the ninth century this movement was to receive an impetus from a series of historical events which churchmen of an earlier time could scarcely have foreseen.

3. Developments in Gaul and Italy

In the Frankish kingdom, by the latter decades of the eighth century, the proprietary church was an established fact. The problem was how to secure its position and its dignity in face of the territorial lord and the ultimate responsibility of the priest to his bishop. Legal enactments aimed at preventing the division of private churches amongst co-heirs. A priest might not be appointed without the bishop's approval nor dismissed by the owner of the church which he served. A priest must attend diocesan synods and render yearly to the bishop an account of his work. Under Louis the Pious (813–40) and Lothair I (840–55) there were efforts to abolish the proprietary system completely, but the influence of the ubiquitous manorial lords brought these to nothing. In due course the system secured legal recognition.

The principal role continued to be exercised by the "mother" churches with their various chapels around them. Thus Hincmar, Archbishop of Rheims, in 858 issued articles of inquiry "per singulas matrices ecclesias, et per capellas". Those who normally worshipped in an oratory or chapel were enjoined to resort to the mother church on great feasts like Easter and Pentecost. The mother churches were otherwise known as "public" churches, or *plebes,* in contrast with the oratories of the private estates; or as "baptisteries", where baptism was administered on behalf of the whole *parochia* or surrrounding area. The general function of these churches in the life of the Christian body is excellently stated by Amulo, Archbishop of Lyons during the middle years of the ninth century, in words which still carry force in an age like our

34

own when many are confused and anxious over the role of the parish church. In the course of a letter to a fellow prelate he maintains that the people should be loyal to their accustomed "parishes and churches", where they receive "the body and blood of the Lord, hear solemn masses, obtain priestly penance and sick visitation, and burial in death, where they are enjoined to offer their tithes and first-fruits, where they rejoice that their children receive the grace of baptism, where they hear God's word and receive instruction in moral duties".

But in the same century privately founded churches were becoming increasingly common; and as time went on there inevitably arose a demand for greater privileges for such churches, a demand too strong for the bishops to resist. At the council of Aachen in 816, shortly after the accession of Louis the Pious, several canons were enacted relating to churches founded privately. Priests might be neither appointed to them nor removed from them without the bishop's approval. On the other hand, the bishop was not to refuse a priest presented by a lay owner, provided the priest was by his life and doctrine a satisfactory candidate. Each church should have its priest, though the means for his support must be guaranteed. The council also decreed that in freshly peopled areas new churches founded within them should have the tithes of those areas, a provision which meant that founders of new churches could grant tithes to them, ignoring the older rights of the baptismal churches.

Legislation of this kind encouraged the establishment of local rural parishes, which by stages were granted by episcopal authority the right to the various sacraments and their own burial-grounds. The council of Toulouse (844) decreed that should a population be so far distant from the "principal church" that the women, children, and infirm could not get conveniently to it, though not so far as to prevent a priest of that church from getting to them, an altar was to be set up where he might minister. But if this were not convenient, or the people were not satisfied with such an arrangement, the parish might be divided and facilities made available for worshippers to have their own priest on the spot.

Broadly, the same ideas were being worked out in Italy. A landmark in Italian history was the fall of the Lombardic kingdom in 774, when Charlemagne asserted his rule in the peninsula and adopted the title *Rex Francorum et Langobardorum*. From now on there were two great powers, the Empire and the papacy, which were to influence profoundly the history of western Europe for centuries to come. Not least, the supremacy of the Franks was to have its effect on the evolution of parishes. An impetus was given to the establishment of proprietary churches in Italy, and to the idea of individual parish churches, each serving a small district or village.

The baptismal churches, which had been the basic unit of pastoral care during the Lombardic period, of course remained. The synod of Pavia half-way through the ninth century sought to define their position. The baptistery remains the principal church of a surrounding group. The wide powers of the archpriest are recognized, particularly in regard to the administration of penance throughout the villages of the district. The term "archpriest", though long known in Gaul, makes its first appearance in Italy about this time. He is chosen by the clergy of the baptistery themselves from amongst their own number, and their choice is approved by the laity. If the right man cannot be found locally, the bishop will help by appointing someone from the diocesan clergy. Other Italian documents of the ninth century and later show that this practice was well known in Italy.

One does not assume, however, that the clergy of the baptismal church and its dependent chapels necessarily formed a corporate group, sharing a common life. In Lombardic Italy this may well have been so, the oratory or chapel priests saying mass and exercising sacerdotal functions in their respective villages, though otherwise normally making their abode with the rector at the baptistery. But practical considerations, as a rule, must have made a real common life for the parochial clergy difficult of achievement. If they were true pastors, they would inevitably find their main preoccupation in the care of their people, with whom they would wish to spend their time rather than in "fellowship" with their brother clergy. Legislators and reformers saw things differently; their aim was that all clergy, even in the rural areas, should live canonically or corporately. But the increasing attachment of the rural folk to Christianity would call for priests willing to exercise a more personal ministry, caring at first hand for the souls of those committed to their charge.

Theorists and legislators had a hard task and the parishes were never susceptible to a general rule. There were cases of churches becoming virtually family possessions, as at Saesto, in the Lucca diocese, where the rectorship passed from father to son through three generations. Bishops sometimes offended in keeping a parish without a rector as long as possible in order to appropriate the revenues, an abuse which was condemned by the synod of Milan in 864. But it was above all the steady withdrawal in the Dark Ages of the richer folk to their country estates which spelt the decline of the central church. In earlier times, when the Roman Empire retained its old civilization and culture, the cities were replete with prosperous households. It was in fact in the houses of well-to-do urban Christians that many apostolic and sub-apostolic congregations had been accustomed to assemble. But now, with the breakdown of the old, rich city life, the influential families lived for the greater part of their time in their country villas. Such families insisted on their own oratories and made but little use of the public baptisteries. Legislators might deplore this tendency, so inimical to the ideal of the Christian common life, but there was little they could do about it. As so often, the facts of life were too strong for the theorist and "man of principle".

One of our most fortunate survivals is a large collection of documents relating to the rural churches of Lucca, in Tuscany, from the early years of the eighth to the close of the tenth centuries. Of special importance are the charters of investiture

by which the rectors received their parishes at the hands of the
bishops of Lucca. The appointment of a rector was in the
form of a lease of a church with its property, a rent being
paid over to the bishop. This was in accordance with normal
practice of agrarian tenure in northern Italy. A priest received
his church conditionally on administering the sacraments within it, in much the same way as an ordinary tenant took a
holding with the undertaking that he would attend to its
essential agricultural work (in person or otherwise). The more
lowly kind of tenant was obliged to reside personally on his
holding, others being free from such restriction and not com-
pelled to render services to the lord. It would seem that in
course of time in the Lucca diocese the usual practice was for
parish priests to hold their churches in the "unrestricted" form
of tenure. That is to say, they were not obliged to minister
personally in their churches should they prefer to depute their
spiritual tasks to other clergymen. Moreover, they might lease
their church land or revenues to their own tenants. The
churches concerned in these contractual agreements between
the Lucca bishops and their rectors were of course the official
"public" or baptismal establishments. Each of these churches
had its land or glebe, and also held the tithes payable by worshippers at the baptismal church itself or at its subsidiary
chapels. One large and very well endowed baptistery,
Quarantiana, received tithes from as many as thirty-nine
villages. So prosperous did some rectors become that they
were even able to lease part of their revenues to laymen by
contracts of their own.

By *c.* 900 church property and revenues in Italy had become
a tempting prize for the aristocratic and military classes, and
tithes and offerings intended in the first place for the clergy
and the maintenance of religious and charitable work were
finding their way into the pockets of the ruling laity. By this
time no fewer than nineteen parishes in the Lucca diocese were
in the possession of laymen. As offerings were no longer simply
the result of popular piety but a compulsory levy of one-tenth
on all farm produce, the churches were much richer than in

earlier days and more liable to the attention of powerful magnates.

In effect, there were in ninth-century Italy two systems of
churches—the episcopal system comprising the cathedrals and
baptisteries with their oratories, and the lay proprietary
system. The coming of Frankish rule gave a strong encouragement to the latter. In 826 it was recognized by law. That is
to say, the lay proprietors were now conceded rights over their
churches provided that the officiating priests were installed
by the bishops. The right of such churches, however, to their
own fonts and to the possession of tithes was persistently
resisted by the bishops, if not always with conspicuous success.
Such privileges belonged properly only to the baptisteries.

Subsequently, with the breakdown of the Carolingian
Empire, there was a period of confusion, order being restored
with the arrival in Italy of Otto I, in 962, at the invitation of
the papacy. Under Ottonian rule the Italian bishops became a
main concern of the reigning power and increasingly secular,
holding their possessions of the emperor through feudal obligation. They themselves had their feudal vassals, the knights,
who emerge in the tenth century clearly as a hereditary class.
It was these men who now became the real power in the
countryside, the dissolution of the Carolingian Empire and
consequent disorder enabling them to fasten their grip on the
districts in which they lived.

The knights naturally coveted the Church's property, and
would appear to have obtained control of much of it with the
approval of the bishops, who needed their loyalty as vassals in
order to meet their own military obligations to the emperor.
During the tenth century many churches and subordinate
chapels, with their various rents and services, went to the lay
magnates, the priest now receiving a rent from the knight in
return for the alienation of his lands and tithes. Sometimes of
course the priest might do well out of such transactions in
terms of immediate gain, but often he would in practice become the mere employee of the local strong man. By the
close of the century the Italian country parishes had been

absorbed into the feudal system, and the commanding position once occupied by the rectors of the baptisteries in the life of the Church was now usurped by laymen. The rise of the local parish church in the West is thus closely associated with the phenomenon of feudalism.

Medieval feudalism had first arisen in the turbulent society of Merovingian Gaul, where men in their need for protection joined the body of a strong man's retainers. Land for maintenance bestowed upon a vassal on particularly favourable terms, with a moderate rent or none at all, and with no obligations of servile labour, came to be known as a *beneficium* —a term which occurs frequently in the Merovingian charters. Professor F. L. Ganshof defined a *beneficium* as "a tenement held on easy terms, or even gratuitously, and which the tenant owes to the generosity of the grantor". It was nearly always held for life, and tended in practice to become hereditary. By the eighth century such "beneficial" holdings were widespread, and from this period onwards the practice of "beneficing" vassals steadily became general. Occasionally a lord might grant an estate to a vassal in full ownership or *proprietas,* but the normal practice was to grant a benefice.

Under feudalism a church came to be looked on as a *beneficium* in the lord's gift, granted in exchange for specific services. With its lands and revenues, the church was part of the landowner's whole estate, disposable by him. In return for his *beneficium* (which, it is important to remember, is quite different from a "stipend") the priest became his lord's "man". This was a far cry from the injunction of Pope Gelasius I (492–6) whereby, though the lord might present the priest, the church and its property must be vested in the bishop. The lord now had full rights of proprietorship. The importance of the ecclesiastical benefice system is that it created within the diocese small independent church units, each centred on a priest and his office. By a formal act of investiture a priest obtained possession of his church and its property for the term of his life. The formal act would consist in some such action as handing over a book, or placing the priest's hand on the church key or bell rope. The priest received his benefice, of course, by virtue of his office and not as a purely personal possession.

By *c.* 1000 the system of private ownership of church properties was general, especially in the lands north of the Alps, though strict churchmen of the reforming school were beginning not only to question it but to oppose it with all the resources at their command. Lay investiture was condemned outright. But the task of wholly removing lay ownership proved eventually impossible, such ownership being simply part of the enormous complex without which early medieval society would have been meaningless.

4. *Parishes in late Saxon England*

In England, private ownership of ecclesiastical buildings was known in the eighth century, as in the case of the two northern churches dedicated by John of Beverley on behalf of Addi and Puch, who were individual laymen. Indeed, the prompt and businesslike way in which Bishop John performed this function, trying to avoid any temptation to waste time over it, almost suggests that it was routine with him. It has sometimes been argued, following the views of Ulrich Stutz, that the proprietary system is in origin Germanic, deriving from the priesthood held by the head of the family. A temple would be built for a household, including the various servants and dependants as well as members of the family itself. With the arrival of the Church the head of the family ceased to exercise priestly functions, though remaining the owner of the local holy place. This is an interesting view, and one is clearly reminded in the same connection of the decisive part played by the secular rulers in the conversion of the Anglo-Saxon kingdoms. But the private church is found at an early date in non-Germanic lands. And, whatever may have been the case with other Germanic countries, in England we have only flimsy evidence for the exercise of sacerdotal functions by landowners.

What would appear certain is that the general insecurity brought about by the great Danish invasions and marauding raids of the ninth century in England had the effect of increasing the importance of the proprietary church. From the first the Vikings directed their attention to the larger churches well stocked with treasures. They sacked Lindisfarne in 793, Jarrow in the following year. The monasteries and minsters underwent such persistent damage at the hands of "the heathen men" that by the latter decades of the ninth century the

42

monasterium, in the eastern kingdoms, had virtually ceased to exist. In the west there may well have been several religious communities still intact but no longer in a position to exert their old influence and leadership. King Alfred himself, as part of his plan of reconstruction in Wessex, had to make a completely fresh start with his two monasteries of Athelney and Shaftesbury. The small churches of the hamlets, on the other hand, held no riches of the sort likely to tempt marauding Danes. Even their chalices, we have reason to believe, were often of wood. And the relative disappearance of the monks and clerical *familiae* must have had the effect of making Christian folk more dependent for their ministrations on the initiative of influential laymen.

In western Europe by the ninth century the *Eigenkirchen-recht,* or the claim of secular men to the ownership of church property, was generally acknowledged. And by the closing years of the century it was probably usual for churches and other ecclesiastical property in England to be in private ownership. From now on each church would have its pro-prietor, as a rule a thegn or manorial lord, though often a bishop, royal person, or ecclesiastical body such as one of the revived or newly founded monasteries. As an instance of this we may take the nunnery of Shaftesbury, which Alfred established and endowed *c.* 875, and where his daughter Aethelgifu took the veil "on account of her bad health". The estates granted included lands in a number of surrounding villages, particularly in Donhead. It may well have been not long after this that the abbey built a church for the benefit of the tenants and serfs on the Donhead estate, where, nestling in its secluded spot by the river Nadder, the present church of Donhead St Andrew includes a tall, narrow arch which is probably of about this time. The owner of a church would be responsible for it, and as interested in it as in any other piece of his property. He might sell it as he chose, or give it away, or mortgage it, or divide its revenues into portions—the development of this habit explains the "fractions" of churches of which we hear at the time of the Norman Conquest. The priest was the lord's man, saying mass as the agricultural serf ploughed the fields. The priest was appointed by the proprietor and was immediately responsible to him. The bishop of the diocese was a distant figure whom the priest seldom saw and scarcely knew save by name, and with whom he had no regular connection apart perhaps from the annual visit in Holy Week to the head minster to collect the holy oils. It is probable that the average bishop was no more interested in the private churches and their worshippers than the saintly John of Beverley showed himself to be, unless of course they were churches (not necessarily within his diocese) of which he himself was proprietor.

We may take it that, when the country emerged late in the ninth century from the long Danish tribulation, it did so with an enhanced sense of the importance of the local church. And with the passing of the years the conception of the "parish priest", living permanently amongst a particular group of people and ministering to them out of personal and intimate knowledge, took root and was accepted as part of social if not of ecclesiastical usage. This is aptly illustrated by a canon of the council which met at Grateley in Hampshire in 928. In cases of penance for perjury, the local priest (*sacerdos locus illius*) is to keep an eye on the penitent's behaviour and report to the bishop. In modern terms, the priest is the offender's "probation officer". Such a canon implies that by this time, in Wessex, most villages or small communities had a priest living on the spot and well acquainted with the people. This was during the reign of Athelstan, a king who was prepared to grant the status of "thegn" to any ceorl who bettered himself to the extent of owning four hides of land complete with church. A humble but enterprising man was in this way encouraged to create an estate for himself out of the waste. Everywhere now the building of village churches was proceeding apace, and the tenth century is probably to be regarded as the great age for the establishment of parish churches as we now understand them, that is to say, churches for a local community with a settled, resident priest, distinct from minster churches with a college of clergy serving a district. A high proportion of our present village and old town churches are undoubtedly descended in an unbroken line (though of course with extensive changes and restoration of the fabric from time to time) from these post-Alfredian foundations. It is to the tenth century that we may ascribe the general introduction of the church tower, which symbolizes the need for security felt by men with bitter memories of the Danes at large in the land. In the tenth century we occasionally encounter priests figuring prominently amongst witnesses and sureties listed at the end of charters. The village priest is becoming a recognized and valued member of rural society. In one document, a late tenth-century grant of land by a certain Aelfhelm to his goldsmith, it is interesting to note that the witnesses include not only what appears to be the local priest but also his son.

By the closing decades of the tenth century a body of law was emerging to cope with the problems created by the growth in the number of churches. At Andover, Hampshire, *c.* 960, King Edgar classified churches in a threefold order—senior churches, churches possessing burial-grounds, and churches without rights of burial. The first class are clearly the old-type minsters, to which men ought to owe their first obedience; the second and third classes represent local churches in varying degrees of self-sufficiency. The same king in his legislation envisages the thegn who has his church on his own land, complete with graveyard. Such a thegn is to pay a third of his tithes to his own church, two-thirds continuing to go to the old minster which hitherto had received the whole.

There was further legislation in the reign of Ethelred, who became king in 979. In his code of 1008 the parish priest, once appointed to his office by the proprietor, cannot be dismissed save with the bishop's consent. An enactment of Aethelred put out at the close of his reign (1014), graded churches according to a scale of penalties prescribed for desecration of their sanctuary rights. It is part of a code which reveals Ethelred legislating consciously as a Christian king with a genuine concern for the Church. The head minster is to be compensated in cases of sanctuary-violation by payment of five pounds, the medium minster ("medemra mynster") by 120 shillings, the smaller minster by 60 shillings (provided this church has a burial-ground), and the "field-church" or chapel (that is, without burial-rights) by 30 shillings. The second class would include most of the older minster churches, the third and fourth the parish churches and chapels now serving village communities. Cnut (1016–35), who based most of his legislation on the enactments of previous kings, repeated Aethelred's 1014 enactment, but described the church of the third class as being one with little divine service. This helps us to see the difference between the traditional minster, with its college of clergy singing the Office in full daily round, and the parish church with a single priest saying mass on Sundays and two or three times in the week, along with the Hours in abbreviated form—perhaps in the vernacular.

Under Edward the Confessor the legal status of parish churches was conceded to all churches which by long custom had the right of administering baptism, marriage, and burial. His great successor William I, in laying down penalties for the violation of churches, drew a distinction between a "mother church" which was a cathedral church or one of monks or religious, and a "mother church of a parish" (*matrix ecclesia parochialis*). He also included within his classification the chapel or *capella*. This enactment is derived ultimately from Ethelred's, but gives greater prominence to the parish church as such. The scale of compensation allowed to the "mother church of a parish" proves that this church corresponds to Ethelred's smaller minster with graveyard.

It is clear that by the eleventh century a local parochial system was taking shape alongside that of the ancient minsters, which, as far as the western half of England was concerned, the Danish wars had weakened but not destroyed. Moreover, as Heinrich Böhmer demonstrated, the English churches by the reign of Edward the Confessor were all proprietary. It

would be virtually impossible to conceive of a church in 1060
as without its owner. The position of the priest himself in
pre-Conquest England, as compared with his fellow on the
Continent, appears to have been good. He was independent,
largely untroubled either by his bishop, who was not always
interested in him, or by his lord provided that he paid the
agreed annual rent, said mass, and dispensed the sacraments.
Except in a few cases he received all the tithes and other
offerings, and farmed his glebe.

We are able to gather something of the duties expected of
the parish priest from three sources of the time, which suggest
that it was largely as a liturgical functionary, as an official
"praying man", that his contemporaries saw him. In the
Canons enacted under King Edgar, ascribed to *c.* 960 and
perhaps compiled by Archbishop Dunstan, it appears that,
ideally at least, the priest is to regard a certain amount of
teaching work as part of his pastoral duties, he himself taking
care to learn a handicraft so that he might in turn teach it
to his people. But the right observance of Sundays and feasts
is emphasized, and the baptism of infants must not be long
delayed. In the celebration of the Eucharist wooden chalices
are not to be used. The parish priest should avoid drunkenness,
and not be tempted to play the part of a tavern-minstrel.
Broadly, we have the same story in a set of canons compiled
a year or two before the year 1000 by Aelfric, monk of Cerne,
for Wulfsige, Bishop of Sherborne, to help him in his dealings
with the Dorset country clergy. Priests, as well as monks, are
to sing the Hours, and should be properly equipped with
liturgical books and vestments. At Sunday mass the parish
priest will expound the gospel, and the Lord's Prayer and
Creed as occasion serves. He must beware of letting any child
die unbaptized, shrive sinners, and minister diligently to the
sick. Let him keep away from taverns. The *Law of the
Northumbrian Priests,* drawn up probably for the York diocese
c. 1020, directs the parish priest to ring the bell at the appointed times and sing the Hours, and to take care that the
festivals and fasts of the Church's year are correctly observed.

He is to see that every child is baptized, and must collect the chrism from the head minster at the customary times (that is, Holy Week). The abuse of celebrating mass with a wooden chalice, or even without wine at all, is condemned. The priest is not to become a gleeman or tavern minstrel. The emphasis on this last point is interesting. Can it be that the priest, as a practised chanter of the Hours, was in some demand as a secular singer also?

It is possible to study the parochial system in late Saxon and early Norman times with reference to some parts of the country fairly fully and precisely, and this is particularly true of the county of Kent, with its dioceses of Canterbury and Rochester.

In the chapter library of Canterbury is a manuscript book to which modern scholars have given the name of *Domesday Monachorum*. Amongst various material in this book, which is the result of a survey of the lands of Christ Church, Canterbury, the section which is relevant to our present inquiry consists of lists of Kentish churches and payments due from them. Though in a handwriting of the early years of the twelfth century, these lists are derived from earlier documents, in some cases Saxon ones. There is first a list of eighty-eight churches, with the amount to be paid by the priest in each case "in pascha", that is (almost certainly) for the holy oils or chrism used in baptisms and customarily collected after ceremonial consecration in the cathedral on Maundy Thursday. The payments are assessed on a unit of 7d; the smaller churches actually pay this sum, the others as a rule in the large multiple of 28d.

With the list of eighty-eight churches is to be associated a shorter list which follows later in *Domesday Monachorum*. This begins with the statement: "This is the institution before the arrival of lord Lanfranc, archbishop". It then lists again the first few names, in exactly the same order, of the "chrism" list, with the amount of dues in kind, mostly in honey, lamb, or wine, from each church. But after proceeding as far as the fourteenth name in the original list, the scribe breaks off, with the observation that "Lanfranc of blessed memory ordained and instituted as afore written". The inference clearly is that in pre-Conquest times the churches paid their chrism fees in kind, but that Lanfranc commuted these for the much more convenient method of payment in money.

In *Domesday Monachorum* is another list, which is the more interesting to the modern mind with its hankering after unions and amalgamations. It is a list of churches arranged in twelve groups, each centred on a senior church. The twelve principal churches, with the numbers of churches "pertaining" to them, are: St Martin-le-Grand, Dover (19), a secular collegiate church (on the site of the present Dover market-place) which was later to become an Augustinian priory and eventually Benedictine; Folkestone (10); Lympne (22), for the parishes of Romney Marsh; Lyminge (10); Milton Regis (10); Newington (7); Teynham (4); Wingham (6); Maidstone (17); Wye (8); Charing (1); an unnamed church (10). These were not rural deaneries, as some students have mistakenly seen them and as many modern readers might be tempted to assume, but rather a development from the earlier minster system, which was something quite different. Some of the churches in the various "groups" are not native, as it were. Thus, one of the churches pertaining to Dover is actually in Folkestone. It would not appear that the groups are the result of conscious efforts towards administrative efficiency and convenience. The central churches are distributed over the diocese very unevenly. The *Domesday Monachorum* list shows signs of being a copy of an Anglo-Saxon list, and the arrangements generally of pre-Conquest origin. We know that the Saxons were somewhat casual in their organization, in contrast with the more tidy-minded Normans. As indication of the Saxon origin of the list is the name Sexburgamynster, applied to Minster-in-Sheppey. Queen Sexburga was wife of Eorconbert, King of Kent 640–64, and traditional founder of a minster in Sheppey. If this list had been drawn up in the first place by a Norman ecclesiastic, it is unlikely that he

would have used such a title for a church or village, as the
conquerors studiously avoided the cult of Saxon saints.

Dover, Folkestone, and Lyminge had been ecclesiastical
centres from as early as the seventh century, and it is known
that in the ninth century each of the three churches still
had a community of clerks serving its surrounding district or
parochia. There were also some other early minster-centres
in Kent, as we have seen, but these do not figure in *Domesday
Monachorum* as senior churches of groups. The Danish ninth-
century wars account for the disappearance of some of these
minsters. Kent suffered very heavily during this time. We
read how Coenwulf, King of Mercia, in 804 along with
Cuthred, King of Kent, made a grant of six acres of land in
the city of Canterbury to Selethryth, abbess of Lyminge, and
her nuns, to serve as a refuge in case of necessity. This must
clearly have been in connection with the Viking raids on the
eastern and southern coasts of England, which began with a
descent on Portland in 787, and included the sack of Lindisfarne and Jarrow a few years later. The raiders were especially
interested in religious houses on or near the coast. The
Anglo-Saxon Chronicle records that in 835 the "heathen men"
ravaged the Isle of Sheppey. About half-way through the
century they spent a whole winter in Thanet and then, sailing
into the Thames mouth with 350 ships, stormed Canterbury
and London. Dover, Folkestone, and Lyminge probably also
suffered from the Danes, and a charter of Athelstan in 927
was to grant to Christchurch, Canterbury, some land at
Folkestone "ubi quondam fuit monasterium", a religious
institution which, the king says, had been destroyed by
heathens. It is clear that the Kentish minster-centres as a
whole came to grief during the great Danish terror. Of the
eight original ecclesiastical centres of the Canterbury diocese,
only Dover, Folkestone, and Lyminge had recovered sufficiently to become the heads of groups by the Norman Conquest or
some time before. The other churches mentioned in *Domesday
Monachorum* as group-centres were all in places of some
importance, such as royal or ecclesiastical manors, and the

implication is that kings or bishops had established fresh clerical communities or minsters thereon to serve the surrounding districts, as part of a general programme to revive religion after the disasters of the ninth century. Thus, some of the places significantly have connections with Canterbury, and in the Conqueror's Survey of 1086 Milton Regis appears as a royal property of long standing. Lyminge was important as a centre of estate administration, where the revenues of adjacent lands were paid in; this would commend it as a centre of church administration also, and the 1086 Survey informs us that there were seven priests there.

Of the actual origin of most of the lesser Kentish churches there is scarcely a hint. The fact that they are somewhat haphazardly and irregularly arranged suggests that they were evolved gradually and as a result of private enterprise. Such can occasionally be gathered from the very names of the dependent churches. Thus, one of the churches in the Lympne group is listed as Aelsiescirce, which is identified with Eastbridge, known to have been held by one Aelsi in the Confessor's reign. Again, Blacemannescirce, in the same group, is the modern Blackmanstone, and the founder must be the Blaceman who held land in the Lympne vicinity, also in Edward the Confessor's reign. In the same group is listed Demancirce (Dymchurch), and Orgarescirce (Orgarswick), which would appear to be churches of private foundation. Such instances remind us of pagan place-names like Peper Harow, "Peper's sanctuary", and Cusanweoh, "Cusa's shrine", both in Surrey. Here is about the only evidence we have of the proprietary church as a continuance of the Germanic private temple in this country. In the same connection Ealham (taken to be the modern Alkham), a church in the Folkestone group, is of interest. The name is probably to be derived ultimately from the Old English "ealh", temple, and suggests a Saxon church retaining a memory of its pagan forbear. Another name, Woodchurch, applied to two Kentish churches, is also of no small interest—it is presumptive evidence that by now most churches were being built of more

durable materials than timber. Men saw the local parish church
as something which had come to stay.

Another point worthy of notice emerges from a comparison
of the two lists of churches in *Domesday Monachorum*. Of
the twelve central churches of the "group" list, ten also appear
in the "fee" list, and all these are assessed at a particularly
high figure. On the other hand none of their dependent
churches appear in the "fee" list. The conclusion is that the
minster church paid its fees for the holy oils to Canterbury
not only on its own behalf but for its dependants, subsequently
recouping itself from the latter. The comparison also makes it
clear that, alongside the minsters with their groups, there
existed a considerable number of independent local churches.
And as far as the head churches of groups are concerned, even
though they are often referred to as "mother" churches, the
only tangible connection between them and their subordinates
is the annual chrism fee, and we have no evidence that the
clergy consciously worked together in partnership. In other
words, to the local priest the "group" in which he was listed
at Canterbury was a lesser reality than the parish in which he
actually lived and worked. If there was more involved in the
grouping of parishes than the mere payment of fees, we know
nothing of it.

There is a further document, listing the churches of the
bishopric of Rochester, and emphasizing still more strongly
the importance of local parishes by this time. It is the *Textus
Roffensis,* discussed in recent years by Dr Gordon Ward. It
details the payments made by the churches for the holy oils
necessary for baptism, each church paying 9d and each chapel
6d. The amount of chrism fees, we observe, varied from
diocese to diocese in the Old English Church. (In the archdiocese of York at this time the fee was 6d for a church and
4d for a chapel.) The date of the *Textus* is *c.* 1115, but as in
the case of *Domesday Monachorum* it is probably a copy of
an older list. The Rochester list looks like a codification of
existing practice; it is unlikely that many of these churches
and chapels were actually founded by the Normans, though

some no doubt were rebuilt in the period *c.* 1070-1115. The list offers a striking illustration of the extent to which west Kent was supplied with parish churches in the later decades of the Anglo-Saxon Church. No fewer than 152 churches and dependent chapels are listed. Names of the present Rochester diocesan rural deaneries appear in the list, such as Chislehurst, Cliffe-at-Hoo, Gravesend, and Sevenoaks (though simply as churches, not as rural deaneries), besides a number of places which have since vanished. Again there is evidence of the private foundation and ownership of churches, as in the names attached to at least three of them—Ordmaeres circe, Dodes circe, and Deremannes circe, the names probably of Anglo-Saxon thegns. Interesting too is the mention of the churches of St John Baptist and St Botolph at Lullingstone, a place which we know to have been a centre of Christian worship even in Romano-British times. All in all, the Canterbury and Rochester lists together prove the existence of some 400 churches and chapels in Kent by the close of the eleventh century, and it is clear that the vast majority must have been of Saxon foundation. The total number of Kentish parishes today is not substantially greater.

The high incidence of parish or manorial churches in many parts of the country is amply confirmed by William I's *Domesday Book* of 1086. This famous document offers a valuable sight of the lines of church organization towards the close of the eleventh century. It is quite certain, however, that numerous churches were not mentioned in the Survey. For example, though we have proof of about 400 churches in Kent, *Domesday Book* offers evidence of the existence of 186. None the less, it is possible to detect the types of church in many counties. In Surrey and Sussex minster churches of the old kind seem to be holding their own along with the newer parish churches. Broadly, the tendency is for the minster to serve a whole district, corresponding to the hundred, in the older settled regions, whereas in the more sparsely populated areas, recently recovered from forest land, manorial churches or chapels are more usual. As we move further west the

continuing importance of the hundred district, served by a
central church, is probable. Thus, in the hundreds of
Fordingbridge and Ringwood in the county of Hampshire, the
only churches listed in *Domesday Book* are those in Fordingbridge and Ringwood themselves. But the argument from
silence is never more dangerous than when we are studying
church entries in the Conqueror's Survey; and it is clear that
much progress had been made in Hampshire in the founding
of parish churches and chapels. We find in the hundred of
Mainsbridge manorial churches at Hinton Ampner, Botley, and
other places. The church of Mottisfont has no fewer than six
dependent chapels or *capellae*. There is no mention of the
church of Titchfield, though it is clear from the substantial
surviving Anglo-Saxon elements in the present fabric that
it must have existed at the time. In fact many churches now
well known for their pre-Conquest fabric find no place in
Domesday Book. Churches with very poor endowment and
thus of no value for taxation purposes would not be included.
Moreover, in *Domesday Book* a thegn is frequently recorded
as holding lands in several places, a priest and church being
mentioned in connection with the village where the thegn
actually lived and with that village alone. A thegn might
indeed often rest content with building a church in the place
of his customary residence, but it cannot be ruled out that
there would sometimes be churches and priests at the other
villages on his estate. For instance, a certain pre-Conquest
Surrey thegn Erding had churches in three or four villages in
his possession. *Domesday Book* does here emphasize the importance of the proprietary element in parish-church organization. Churches too which belonged to religious houses or
ecclesiastics who had appropriated the revenues would not
be entered. It is for this reason that such famous Anglo-Saxon
churches as Bradford-on-Avon (belonging to the abbess and
convent of Shaftesbury), and Wing (to St Nicholas abbey,
Angers), are absent from the Survey. And it would seem that
the Domesday scribes, in dealing with entries relating to
churches, proceeded along different lines from county to

county. In Suffolk and Huntingdonshire the coverage of churches is so thorough that one presumes it is virtually complete; in some other counties, such as Oxfordshire and Cambridgeshire, Bedfordshire and Hertfordshire, the churches and their priests appear to have been largely ignored.

In Wiltshire several of the hundred-districts were owned by bishops and monasteries, and *Domesday Book* therefore normally makes no reference to churches within them. In other cases we have mention of a single church for a hundred, such as Winterbourne Stoke for the hundred of Dole, Westbury church for Westbury hundred, Heytesbury church for Heytesbury hundred. We may have here minsters of the traditional type still serving a wide district, though elsewhere, in the hundred of Chippenham, there are churches in other places besides Chippenham itself. In Dorset the situation is somewhat complicated by the presence of several well-endowed monasteries—Abbotsbury, Milton, Cranborne, Shaftesbury, Cerne, Wimborne, and Horton—which between them must have owned many churches in the county. The abbey of Fontenelle St Wandrille, near Rouen, also held Dorset possessions, including the church of Whitchurch Canonicorum. This church is of peculiar interest today as containing the only shrine in England left undisturbed by the Reformation—that of St Candida, whom tradition takes to have been a local woman who remained loyal and died a martyr for her faith during the Danish tribulation. The hundred of Gillingham appears to have been served by the minster of St Mary in Gillingham. But in Winfrith hundred, we read of churches at Winfrith Newburgh, Puddletown, and East Chaldon.

The further west we move, the more clearly do we see the old minsters maintaining their position. In Somerset there are borough minsters, and churches at hundred manors, repeatedly only one church being recorded for a hundred-district. St John's, Frome, gives the impression of having been the spiritual centre not only for the town but for the hundred. Moreover, the ample size of the endowments of these churches implies communities of clergy serving them. In Devon and

Cornwall, in 1086, the Church is obviously run in the main
from central churches with colleges of secular canons. For
the latter county eleven collegiate churches are recorded, and
there is no reference to village churches—though one does
not thereby assume, of course, that they did not exist.

In East Anglia, on the other hand, it was the small local
church which by 1086 was the characteristic unit of church
administration. *Domesday Book* has little to offer concerning
the churches of Essex, but such as are mentioned are parish
churches, though St Peter's, Colchester, may have had a
community of priests. In Norfolk and Suffolk a particularly
thorough conquest by the Danes in the ninth century had
virtually wiped out the older ecclesiastical organization. When
the invaders themselves became Christian (and they made
surprisingly good converts) an entirely fresh start had to be
made, and it is clear that little effort was directed towards
reviving the old-fashioned minsters. Parish churches pure and
simple, from the tenth century onwards, became the norm.
These were established in great numbers, in an enthusiastic
wave of church building, in town and country alike. In
Norwich there were at least twenty-five churches and forty-
three chapels; in Thetford at least twelve churches, and in
Ipswich no fewer than eight. In Norfolk, apart from the towns,
mention is made of 217 churches, about one for every three
villages or hamlets in the county; but there is evidence that
this list is incomplete. For example, no reference is made
specifically to a church at Heveningham, though there was a
priest there who said mass three times a week. In Suffolk
there are altogether 639 places of population, from towns to
small hamlets, with churches in connection with 345 of them
apart from those of the towns. In the Stowmarket area almost
every village has its church. In some of the Suffolk entries we
sense the idea of the "parish church" in much the same way
in which it is regarded in our own day in rural England. Thus
we read in some instances of the "village church" (*ecclesia
huius villae*), and elsewhere we have reference to "parishioners" (*parochiani*).

There is another feature of the ecclesiastical arrangements of these two counties which invites special notice. Whereas elsewhere in England the rural churches had been founded invariably by landowners or ecclesiastical bodies, here they were often the work of freemen acting communally. The Vikings were "democratic" men of the boats, with the habit of rowing or fighting as a crew or a team ingrained in them. We seem to see this habit continued in the more pacific work of the founding of churches. In the Norfolk village of Letton the church with twelve acres attached to it was on the holding of a group of nine freemen. Similarly, at Stonham, Suffolk, the land belonging to the church had been given by nine freemen. In East Anglia generally the population was more independent than elsewhere, with more scope for the initiative of humble men and with greater control over the local resources.

In the east midlands, though this region also was largely taken over by the Danes, the older organization does not seem to have vanished as in East Anglia. But here too the parish churches were numerous—quite enough to overshadow the ancient minsters. In the biggest town, Lincoln, recently made the seat of a bishopric, there were five parish churches referred to in *Domesday Book*. These were St Lawrence, St Mary, St Michael, All Saints, and St Peter. The most important of them was St Peter, the property of Earl Roger of Poitou, who in 1094 was to give it along with other English churches to the Benedictines of Sées in Normandy. But there were several other churches, not mentioned in *Domesday Book,* in the city, including a number dedicated to St Peter, always a favourite saint in the Old English Church. They also included the surviving churches of St Mary le Wigford and St Peter at Gowts, both of which have fabrics dating from about this time. A particularly interesting and often quoted case in connection with Lincoln city is a certain Colsuen, who is mentioned in *Domesday Book*. He had thirty-six houses and two churches (without endowment), which he had built on some waste ground granted to him by the king. He possessed scattered estates elsewhere, making him a by no means inconsiderable landowner. As he is not recorded as having had any land at the actual time of the Conquest, and his name is a native English one, there is a strong suspicion that he was a collaborator who found his way into the Conqueror's favour. He seems to have been a plain self-seeker, the two churches on the outskirts of Lincoln being built with an eye to profit. These churches have not been certainly identified, but the estate of which they formed part was on the eastern edge of the city.

In the commercial settlement of Grantham there was one especially well-endowed church, St Wulfran, which with another church of the town was to be made over to Salisbury (Old Sarum) cathedral a few years later. The Salisbury chapter to this day includes Grantham Australis and Grantham Borealis in its list of prebends. In Lincolnshire as a whole there is evidence from *Domesday Book* of some 245 manorial or parish churches, not counting those of the urban areas. But Mr J. W. F. Hill in his study of medieval Lincoln thinks it likely that there were anything from 300 to 400 churches in the county by the year 1100. This does not mean, of course, that there was a sudden outburst of church building in the last decade or two of the century, but that a great many churches were simply not included in the Survey of 1086. In other counties there are minsters at Southwell, Derby, and other centres, though none according to *Domesday Book* (which admittedly has little to say about churches of any kind for the central midlands) in Leicester, Northampton, Oakham, or Cambridge.

In the west midlands the church organization appears to have been a mixed one, with minsters large and small besides many parish churches. But the further west we go the more important is the minster. There is more evidence for collegiate secular churches in this area than anywhere else in late eleventh-century England. In the town of Chester is a group of minsters of secular canons, St Werburgh, St John, and St Mary, but no parish churches of which we know. Shrewsbury is served by groups of secular canons, the titles of whose foundations survive today in the old churches (mostly rebuilt in the eighteenth century) of that picturesque town. There appear to have been no individual parish priests in Shrewsbury. Shropshire generally was still well provided with minsters, as was also Staffordshire, which moreover had the cathedral of Lichfield. In the city of Hereford, besides the cathedral, there were the collegiate churches of St Peter and St Guthlac.

In Worcestershire much of the land was owned by a group of Benedictine abbeys—St Mary Worcester, Evesham, Pershore, Malvern, and Westminster. Minsters had been prominent in the county at an earlier time, but it appears that by now their endowments had fallen to the abbeys, and churches with a single priest were probably more usual than formerly, though actually few churches of any sort for Worcestershire are recorded in 1086. Gloucestershire also may have had many minsters which by this time had been absorbed by the rise of Benedictinism, or had "deteriorated" into parish churches each with a priest or two. *Domesday Book* proves the existence of churches at about fifty-four places in the county, but there were certainly many more.

For Lancashire, very few churches of any sort are returned in *Domesday Book*. But in Yorkshire the minsters include the great names of York, Beverley, and Ripon, and there are many parish churches both in York city and in the rural areas. The York city churches mentioned in *Domesday Book* include St Mary Castlegate, which according to an inscription inside the church was founded jointly by Efrard, Grim, and Aese, who judging by their names must have been Danish citizens. The foundation of St Olave's church in the city is recorded in the Anglo-Saxon Chronicle, *sub anno* 1055; we read that earl Siward died at York in that year, and was interred in the church which he had previously built in the name of God and St Olave and to the honour of God and all saints. William I gave this church, with four acres of land, to Alan, Earl of Richmond, who in his turn presented it to the newly founded abbey of St Mary. In addition to the parish churches of York city included in the Survey, there are others not listed (as

belonging to religious houses), such as the well known St
Michael's, Spurriergate.

How can we sum up the evidence of *Domesday Book*? By
and large it suggests that many minsters were still holding
their own, particularly in the west. But it is also apparent from
the Survey that the parish churches held the real key to the
future, and nowhere is this more evident than in the eastern
counties. In *Domesday Book* the outstanding fact with regard
to the Church's work amongst the people is the parish or
manorial church served by its own priest. Here and there a
priest appears to be serving two, or even three churches, but
this is unusual. Occasionally we encounter a church with two
priests, but this as often as not seems to be an old minster
in process of settling down to a more modest role in the field
of pastoral ministration. The stock formula for entry in
county after county, "ibi ecclesia et presbyter", which occurs
time and again, tells its own story. The parish church and
its priest are becoming part of the English fabric.

The great majority of the churches listed and referred to in
Domesday Book, and in the Canterbury and Rochester chrism-
lists, were of Saxon foundation. But during the time of the
Conquest and for years afterwards the founding of churches
went ahead. Thus, Wulfwig, Bishop of Dorchester 1053–67,
consecrated a church at Studham in Bedfordshire on behalf
of a royal thegn Oswulf and his wife Aethelith. Wulfstan, who
was Bishop of Worcester from 1062 to 1095, encouraged the
building of new churches, establishing some on his own estates
and urging other landowners to do the same. We know of a
church founded by Athelhelm, abbot of Abingdon, at Whistley,
Berkshire, *c.* 1080; and of a church founded or refounded at
Harrow by Lanfranc late in his archiepiscopate. Churches
would often be built because of a real need, as is exemplified
in the case of Whistley. Here the villagers were formerly
parishioners of Sonning which was three miles away on the
other side of a river liable to severe flooding in winter.

Although local churches were steadily increasing, the ancient
minsters were still active in many places, and it would prob-

ably be true to say that by the close of the eleventh century in England the system of pastoral care was a "mixed" one. The tidy classification of the entire land into local parochial divisions each with its rector or vicar assisted in some cases by a curate, lay well in the future.

But meanwhile many of the surviving minsters must have become shadows of their former selves, with the areas of their influence much reduced. The minster of Morville, Shropshire, served by a college of eight canons in the Confessor's time, had only three priests in 1086; most of its landed property had been made over to Shrewsbury abbey, and *Domesday Book* refers to it as a "manorial" church. Many minsters after the Conquest were converted into regular monasteries, while some survived to become the secular colleges of the middle ages. The movement towards the establishment of medieval collegiate churches appears to have already begun late in the tenth century as part of the ecclesiastical revival which characterized those years, and received some encouragement in the reign of the Confessor. It is in the eleventh century that the word *canonicus* is beginning to be applied in its familiar modern sense to a secular clerk on the staff of an important church. There were many such institutions at the time of the Conquest, including the famous churches of Ripon, Beverley, and Southwell, within the archdiocese of York; and there was a particularly thick cluster in the west midlands and along the Welsh borders. As an instance of what might eventually happen to a minster we may take Heytesbury, in the diocese of Salisbury, to which reference has already been made. In 1165 this was to be reconstituted as a college of secular canons, with dependent churches or chapels at Knook, Tetherington, Hill Deverill, and Horningsham. The present parish church of Heytesbury still has collegiate status and is so listed in *Crockford's Clerical Directory*, though its prebends have long been vacant. Meanwhile on the purely parochial level there was by the twelfth century, if not before, a clear distinction between parish churches and chapels. Some of these chapels have since become parish churches in their own right, many have completely disappeared. In the parish of Donhead St Andrew, Wiltshire, it has long been known that in the middle ages there was a dependent chapel in the outlying hamlet of Easton. All traces of this had disappeared until in 1966, during alterations to a barn on Chapel Farm, the voussoir to a twelfth century arch came to light. Instances such as this could no doubt be multiplied. In the totality of the medieval ecclesiastical organization the chapels form an element worthy of more intensive study than has hitherto been bestowed upon it.

5. The Priest and his Living

By many and ingenious ways the Church of the Dark Ages sought to ensure its material position. The blessings it brought to society in the way of culture, learning, and pastoral care had to be paid for, and by the eleventh century what had at first been to a large extent voluntary offerings were virtually levies enforced on all. Though the average parish priest probably seldom at any time received the whole of the emoluments arising from his parish, he figures prominently in any discussion relating to the history of ecclesiastical endowments in England.

The rule of the Roman Church, as put by Gelasius I (492–6), in a letter relating to the revenues of the churches of Lucania, Bruttium, and Sicily, was that the diocesan revenues should be divided into four portions, for the bishop himself, his clergy, the church fabrics, and the poor. This rule, however, was never universally or strictly enforced, and a threefold division was sometimes the practice. Out of his share the bishop would be expected to maintain his *familia*, and (in the case of a threefold division) the fabrics of minsters in his diocese. The parochial clergy received stipends at the bishop's discretion. Or the bishop would have no share at all in the general revenues, receiving instead specified episcopal dues. The money available for the poor would be used for a wide variety of charitable objects, including pilgrims and Christians in captivity as well as the poor and sick. A century after the time of Gelasius, the fourfold rule was pointed out to Augustine by Pope Gregory, though it was actually the threefold division which came to prevail in the Canterbury archdiocese.

In England, plough-alms and soul-scot, though not mentioned until the time of King Athelstan (925–39), were almost as old as Christianity itself. The former was a small charge on each plough-team, payable at Easter. Soul-scot looks very much like a continuation of the primitive pagan practice of depositing the deceased's treasures, such as his weapons and jewellery, in his grave. It continued throughout the middle ages as the "mortuary" gift to the priest, and survives, in effect, in the modern burial fee. More important than either of these two sources of revenue was the church-scot, which is first met with in the laws of Ine, King of Wessex 688–726. It was payable at Martinmas, by all freemen possessed of an agricultural holding, as a rule in grain. Its payment was enforced by King Edmund and King Edgar in the tenth century, by which time it was reserved for the ancient minsters to whom it had originally belonged. It was always in kind, though the amount payable varied from place to place.

But it was above all the tithe which provided the sinews to enable the Church to do its work in the world. The doctrine that all men should pay a tithe of their possessions to the work of God is traceable to the Old Testament, where we read that Abraham gave tithes to Melchizedek, king of Salem, and that Jacob vowed to the Lord the tithe of all his substance which he might acquire in Mesopotamia. According to Leviticus 27. 30–32, all the tithes of the land, including fruit-trees, and of herds and flocks, are devoted to the Lord. We do not read in the New Testament, however, that our Lord enjoined the paying of tithes; on the contrary, he referred disparagingly to the punctilious payment of tithes on the part of those who neglected the more important points of the law. Though such fathers as Jerome and Augustine recommended the dedication by Christians of a tenth of their substance to God, the fifth-century canon law of the Roman Church does not mention tithes, and it was not for a century or more that their payment was being seriously urged by the Church as a religious duty. The Carolingians, in the latter decades of the eighth century, made the tithe compulsory.

Similarly in England, the payment of tithes came but gradually. In the first century of the English Church's history it was regarded as a duty incumbent on Christian men, who might however devote their tithe offerings to any worthy object at their discretion. Tithe is first actually mentioned by Theodore, who ruled that it should be paid to pilgrims, the poor, and the donor's own church. Bede writes approvingly of the gift of tithes of food and clothes to the poor. Boniface, writing to Cuthbert, Archbishop of Canterbury, in 746–7, refers to the bishops as receiving tithes and offerings from their people. Later in the same century, English ecclesiastical councils enjoined the payment of tithes—but there was still no effort on the part of the kings to enforce it. Alfred did not do so, though he was fully aware of the Old Testament precedent for it. It was in the tenth century that tithes were definitely enjoined as obligatory, by secular authority. Athelstan and Edmund both went a long way in this direction; and then Edgar in his enactments at Andover (959–63) laid down measures for the enforcement of tithes throughout England. The reeves are to seize one-tenth of a defaulter's tithable property on behalf of the minster church; four-fifths will be divided between the bishop and the defaulter's lord, the remaining tenth will be left to the culprit. These were severe penalties and one wonders how vigorously they were ever enforced. The important point is that the secular power is at last endeavouring to compel the payment of tithes, which are no longer simply a pious, voluntary offering. And whereas originally the tithe was disposable at the donor's discretion, and might be given to the poor and to such objects as the redemption of captives, in Edgar's code it is specifically linked with the needs of the "parochial" system. The tithe belongs rightly to the old minsters, that is, to the minsters in whose territorial jurisdiction the tithepayer's land at first lay. But if a proprietor has a church complete with graveyard, he shall give a third of his tithes to this church, the remaining two-thirds still going to the minster. If the church is without graveyard, its lord shall pay the priest anything he chooses after he has met his

obligations to the minster. Edgar's code also orders the payment of all church-scot to the old minster, "from every free
hearth", as well as other dues, such as the penny from every
household on St Peter's day.

Domesday Book seldom refers to the tithe, church-scot, or
other dues of this sort, though in the case of East Anglia it is
informative as to the other great source of ecclesiastical income, namely glebe. It appears normal in Suffolk, for example,
for the village church to have its landed possessions. The
church of Long Melford had as much as 240 acres, though
this was exceptional, an endowment of about thirty acres being
more usual. Reginald Lennard points out that similar conditions probably prevailed elsewhere in England, Suffolk and
Norfolk simply being noteworthy for the fullness with which
the facts are recorded. In this Survey of 1086 we have a clear
sight of the priest as cultivator of the soil, as at home with his
team of plough-oxen as in the sanctuary of his church. From
his glebe and tithe, and other dues such as church-scot and
plough-alms, he has his "living", varying in amount from
village to village and not necessarily related to the size of the
population to whom he ministers. He does not always receive
the whole of the tithe payable from his parish, two-thirds of it
going to the original minster. In some cases he may not receive
any tithe at all. For the use of the glebe he pays rent to the
proprietor of his church. And non-resident incumbents are by
now becoming a feature of the ecclesiastical scene, some of
the wealthier churches being held by churchmen who put in
chaplains, at a wage, to do their pastoral work for them. It is
impossible to define clearly the nature and incidence of
parochial endowments at this time. And how varied these
could be is shown by a charter of the years just following the
Conquest, relating to the church of Lambourn, in Berkshire.
The charter lists the church's endowments, which include, besides a full hide (about a hundred acres) of land, such items as
the tenth lamb and the tenth young pig, a wey of cheese at
Michaelmas, fifteen pence at Easter, pasture for the priest's
oxen, cattle, and sheep, as well as for his two horses and for

forty swine in the woods and open country, and wood for his fire. In addition there were the customary tithes of harvest-corn. This was clearly a "good living", and the church would seem to have been one of the old minsters. The charter refers to the "parish and hundred" of Lambourn, and to the church itself as a "minster". It is possible that the five priests (Croc, Harding, Werman, Walter, and Theodric) and one deacon (Walter), whose names appear as witnesses to the document, are the clerical staff, the senior priest being Croc, whose name heads the list.

It is obviously not easy to gather from *Domesday Book* the true social and economic position of the parochial clergy. There are many anomalies and variations. Some clergy held a good position, with their tenants and even serfs. The priest of Hinton Martell, Dorset, held two ploughs, four *villani* and a couple of bordars, a mill, eleven acres of meadow, extensive woodland, and several houses in nearby Wimborne. But "fat" livings were tending to get into the hands of the rapidly rising class of absentee clerks engaged in administrative work; and on the whole those who bore the burden and heat of the day in the parishes appear to have been simple members of the peasant class. In most cases the village priest was probably on about the same level as the *villanus*. Some years after 1086, according to a survey of the estates of Shaftesbury abbey, we find the priest of the Wiltshire village of Berwick St Leonard (where the ancient church has only recently been closed for public worship) enjoying as his glebe half a hide of land, sufficient to support fifteen cattle, sixty sheep, three horses, and fifteen swine. His name was Wulfric. There were probably parish priests all over the country with a similarly modest competence. In many cases the priest would be expected to perform some service in return for his living to the proprietor. A well-known instance of this is in Herefordshire, where three priests had to serve as royal messengers in Wales and say two masses each week on behalf of the king. This was doubtless exceptional, though we may well believe that many a priest was obliged to say the offices in the manor house of a proprietary lord disinclined to attend his parish church. We need not suppose that the priest was usually required to render manual service on his lord's farm-lands.

We can never know what manner of men were the parochial clergy of the late Saxon and early Norman periods. Chroniclers were not interested in them. The very names of most of them have passed away—the episcopal registers from which we derive the "lists of rectors" hanging today on the walls of numerous churches belong to a later stage in the middle ages. There is much incidental evidence, however, to suggest that a high proportion of the parish priests were married. The propriety of this was probably not over-questioned by the laity, though strict ecclesiastics frowned on it or even denounced it. The novice-master of Cerne abbey, Aelfric, who shortly before 1000 wrote his *Catholic Homilies* in the vernacular to provide a set of sermons for Sundays and festivals on behalf of the Dorset "upland" clergy, was sternly opposed to clerical marriage. The *Law of the Northumbrian Priests, c.* 1020, acknowledges that a priest may marry, but the compiler cannot bring himself to write of a true wife and refers to the priest's "woman". Aethelred II legislated against the practice; and Wulfstan II, Bishop of Worcester, ordered his clergy to choose between their churches and their wives. Gregory VII (Hildebrand) in synod at Rome in 1075 insisted on all priests putting away their wives. In the following year Archbishop Lanfranc, in his Winchester council, tried to meet the problem half-way by allowing married parish priests to retain their wives, though requiring all future ordinations to be accompanied by a vow of celibacy. A series of twelfth-century councils found it necessary to continue the assault on priestly marriage in England, though without entire success. The habit of marriage was so ingrained amongst the English clergy that hereditary livings appear to have been common. The famous Cistercian, Aelred of Rievaulx, who was born in 1110, came of a line of learned and highly respectable married priests in Northumbria. The York city church of St Denis Walmgate remained hereditary until *c.* 1170. At the other end of England, the parish priest of Haselbury in Somerset, Brichtric by name, was a married priest so devout that after a morning in church he would hurry home on his horse to dinner, and then ride back to resume his psalmody. We have a pleasing glimpse of his wife Godida sewing a linen alb for an anchorite in the parish. Presumably she looked after her husband's vestments as well. Brichtric's son Osbern served him at mass, and eventually succeeded him as priest of the parish.

6. Rectors and Vicars

In the Dark Ages it was not uncommon on the Continent for a lay lord to bestow the revenues of a church in his ownership on whom or what he willed, as if they were absolutely his property. The tithes were not regarded as belonging exclusively to spiritual concerns, and it was not unknown for a lord to settle some of the emoluments on close relatives, even his wife. But from the tenth century onwards the most usual recipients of such generosity were the monasteries, now assuming a place of renewed importance in the Church's life. It was a generosity at the expense of the parochial clergy and normally not involving any sacrifice on the donor's part, except in so far as he himself was contributing to the tithes concerned. For such donations episcopal approval does not seem to have been required at first, but was increasingly insisted on from *c*. 1000 onwards.

The eleventh and twelfth centuries were an age of religious revival, pious fervour showing itself in such phenomena as the crusades and the foundation of monasteries. Under the prevailing enthusiasm monastic houses were growing up like mushrooms, in England as elsewhere in western Europe. But monasteries, especially well-ordered and carefully planned ones of the Benedictine type, were expensive establishments. They had to be paid for and the money could only be forthcoming from the parishes. The simple truth is not invariably realized that the total wealth of the Church was that of the combined tithes, offerings, and dues of all the parish churches. It was thus that the practice of "appropriating" churches by the monasteries and other ecclesiastical bodies or persons came into being, characterizing what is virtually the final stage in the evolution of the classical parochial system, when priests in full receipt of the income of their churches were known as rectors, whereas the appropriated church was served by a priest called the vicar and receiving a suitable share of the endowments.

As early as the ninth century monasteries here and there on the Continent appear to have owned parochial endowments. There would as yet, however, have been no suggestion of a vicar with his clearly defined position and security. The French scholar Imbart de la Tour found his earliest reference to a vicar in a document of 926, in France, where a certain ecclesiastic presented to a church put in a *vicarius sacerdos* to attend to the spiritual duties. In the tenth century the granting of parish churches with their endowments to monasteries was a fairly regular practice on the Continent, and from the eleventh century it increased. It was justified on the grounds that the monks are to be included amongst the poor, who have a traditional and canonical claim on the tithes. The monks are men who have left all to follow the poor Christ, and for this reason deserve some share of the good things which admittedly in the first place are due to those who actually do Christ's work in the world, that is to say the parish clergy. The early Cistercians were to have qualms over this argument, refusing to touch parochial endowments, though the Benedictines and Cluniacs had no such scruples.

In England, the ownership of churches by monasteries before the Conquest was relatively rare. The idea that parochial endowments could be diverted to other uses than that of the support of the local priest and church had not yet really become current, and the gift of a church therefore carried with it small pecuniary advantage. The view that possession of a church was a financial asset to be exploited was not seriously held until the reign of the Confessor. But different ideas prevailed on the Continent, and after the Conquest the new manorial lords from Normandy often gave the churches in their possession, along with the endowments, to religious foundations which they favoured, including abbeys abroad such as Mont St Michael and Bec. There was little or no episcopal opposition to this development, and indeed the bishops may well have thought that the churches would be likely to be better cared for spiritually when in monastic ownership. Monastic possession was in line with the principles of the Gregorian reform movement, which objected to lay ownership of churches. But it would appear that in practice churches acquired by the monasteries simply came to be cared for by secular priests enjoying a small portion of the parochial income, not by the monks themselves. To the monastic chapters, the churches acquired by them were invariably a source of income rather than a spiritual responsibility. In the twelfth century vast numbers of English churches were made over to religious houses in England and Normandy; and in addition other monasteries received separate grants of tithes from parochial revenues in the form of annual pensions, as when the abbey of Sées secured pensions from the Sussex churches of Harting and Rogate. Churches were also given to cathedral chapters from an early post-Conquest time; thus the rich Wiltshire church of Mere fell to the Salisbury chapter. Moreover, *Domesday Book* reveals that churches were being bestowed after the Conqueror's arrival on individual ecclesiastics important to him in administrative work, such as the priest Rainbald, who was chancellor under the king. Rainbald, the "first great pluralist", held many well-endowed livings in the west country.

In this connection mention might here be made of the prebendal churches, that is to say, parish churches which came to be appropriated to prebends in cathedrals and other great churches. In such cases the individual prebendary, not the dean and chapter, was the rector. Thus, four churches in the Lincoln diocese provided the endowment for a number of prebends in Salisbury cathedral. The two Grantham churches to which we have already referred (p. 58) were part of the cathedral's original endowments. In addition there were the churches of Bricklesworth (Brixworth), Northamptonshire, and Shipton, Oxfordshire, which were made over to Salisbury (Old Sarum) cathedral early in the twelfth century, to provide the income for a prebend. Later, during the episcopate of Richard Poore (1217–29), the income was separated to provide for two prebends; and in 1240 the church of Bricklesworth was specifically assigned to the chancellorship of the cathedral, on the petition of Adam de Esseby, then holder of the office. From Adam's time until well into the nineteenth century the chancellor of Salisbury held the gift of the parish of Brixworth —famous today for its splendid Anglo-Saxon church.

There were other benefices of a similar type, including a group in the Salisbury diocese which Bishop Simon (1297– 1315) was to find awkward and difficult to classify. The group consisted of prebendal churches held by the five great Wessex nunneries (all Benedictine) of Shaftesbury, Wilton, Romsey, Wherwell, and St Mary's, Winchester—the last three houses being within the Winchester diocese. The group by *c.* 1300 included the prebendal churches of Iwerne Minster and Gillingham (belonging to Shaftesbury), Imber and Urchfont (belonging to Romsey and St Mary's, Winchester, respectively), and various others. The church of Chalke (Broad-chalke) was prebendal to Wilton, where the prebendary (rector of Chalke) was expected to reside as closely as possible, to help the nuns with his advice if they should need it. He had, however, in the monastery a priest-vicar to say mass on his behalf, as well as three "perpetual vicars" holding the cure of souls in Chalke and four chapels dependent upon it. Two of these chapels, Bowerchalke and Alvediston, survive today as parish churches. But although in theory the holders of the "conventual" prebendal churches were bound to reside, at least sometimes, in their respective nunneries, in practice they tended to be absentees with legal or academic qualifications, often engaged in the royal service. As such they could, of course, be extremely useful to the nuns, even though they were seldom seen by them. In this, as in other ways, appropriated churches played their necessary part in the general running and organization of the early medieval Church.

Such churches in England came to be served by "vicars". As early as the first few years of the twelfth century, when the church of Westfield was appropriated to Battle abbey, in the diocese of Chichester, the priest who is to serve the church is called the vicar. Though he is not said to have had his specified portion of the tithes, he is properly instituted after formal presentation. There was also a parochial vicar in Pershore in 1147. But regularized vicarages in the twelfth century were comparatively rare, the vicar normally being appointed not according to the rules of a general system but as a particular occasion served. The vicar usually had no real security of tenure.

The religious were men vowed to withdrawal from the world, and even if they had desired to do so would have been canonically unable to serve the cures of the churches of which they had obtained possession. The Lateran council of 1123 in fact forbade monks to serve as parish priests, and the 1179 Lateran council enjoined monasteries to present priests to the bishop on behalf of their churches. In the thirteenth century it was still very uncommon for monks to serve their churches in person, though slightly more usual later in the middle ages. Only the Austin and especially the Praemonstratensian canons regarded pastoral work as compatible with their profession, but even they did not often serve parishes.

In 1172, a council at Avranches under Alexander III stipulated that vicars were not to be appointed for fixed terms only but must have greater security and the receipt of one-third of the revenues. This was a real advance. But it was Innocent III who became the great champion of the parish priest. He denounced the bestowal of tithes by lay lords on non-parochial objects or persons. They who do the work should receive the pay. And in the famous Fourth Lateran Council of 1215 (canon 32) held under the same pope, it was enacted that the custom must be abandoned whereby "patrons of parish churches, and certain other persons who claim the profits for themselves, leave to the priests deputed to the service of them, so small a portion that they cannot be rightly sustained. . . . We have ordained that by a custom of the bishop or patron a sufficient portion be assigned to the priest".

The rector of a parish, when not himself residing, must see that a vicar, with his guaranteed portion of the revenues, is to be instituted. The whole point about this canon (which is the lynch-pin of the entire medieval vicarage system) is that a vicar is no mere employee in receipt of a wage and removable at will, but a beneficed priest with his freehold and specified endowment, and instituted by the bishop. He cannot be removed save for crimes or grave dereliction of duty, and then only by judicial procedure. On his part the priest accepts the obligation to continuous residence in his benefice. Already in the twelfth century many vicars had held their own separate endowments, but from now on they could claim these endowments as of right in canon law.

After the Fourth Lateran Council there was a big increase in the number of vicarages. In the Lincoln diocese under Bishop Hugh de Welles (1209–35) scarcely fewer than 300 are recorded, and throughout the English Church as a whole the ordination of vicarages now proceeded apace. There was no hard and fast rule as to the proportion of the revenues to be assigned to the vicar, but these tended to approximate to a third of the total income of the church. Generally, the vicar would have a house and garden, the offerings of his parishioners, and the lesser tithes. Various burdens, such as the maintenance of assistant clerks, and the payment of synodals and visitation fees, were sometimes borne by the vicar, sometimes shared between him and the appropriator. Upkeep of the chancel was the responsibility of the appropriator, as rector. According to an enactment of the council of Oxford in 1222 held under the presidency of Archbishop Stephen Langton, the vicar's income was to be not less than five marks (£3 6s 8d), except in the case of very poor livings in Wales. Several vicarages in the thirteenth century were actually well above this amount; but the large majority would appear to have been between £3 and £4 a year, about the same as the wages of a contemporary artisan. Then, as today in the Church of England, the "minimum" income for most vicars tended to be the maximum that they could hope

for. Cardinal Otto, who visited England in 1237, ordained
that a vicar on institution must already be a deacon and if
not a priest must proceed to priestly orders within a year.
Thirty years later, Cardinal Ottobon at the council of London
insisted on competent provision for vicars, including suitable
houses. That appropriations were getting rather out of hand
is clear from a papal mandate of 1261, during the pontificate
of Alexander IV, to the bishops of Salisbury, Coventry and
Lichfield, Worcester, Lincoln, and Llandaff. The mandate
objects to the greediness of the religious in persistently seeking
churches, leading to a diminution of divine service in such
churches, a narrowing of the field of episcopal authority, and
of the opportunities for poor but able priests to secure
promotion.

It was the second General Council of Lyons, in 1247, which
laid down what may be regarded as the ultimate conditions
for the institution of a parochial incumbent. Not less than
twenty-five years old, and of suitable education and character,
he must reside personally on his benefice, though may be
permitted by his bishop to be non-resident for stated intervals.
Should a patron fail to present an incumbent to a vacant
benefice within six months, the presentation will pass for that
term to the bishop.

By the close of the thirteenth century it is likely that there
were about 9,000 or more parishes in the English Church,
and of these at least 1,500 are known to have been vicarages.
Appropriations continued in the fourteenth century, and even
in the fifteenth—when they were usually for the benefit of a
hospital, chantry foundation, or educational establishment
rather than a monastery. In the *Valor Ecclesiasticus* of 1535,
of the 8,838 parishes actually recorded, just over a third are
vicarages. The vicars were a fairly homogeneous class, except
in unusual cases personally resident in their parishes. One
must not assume that they were all insignificant men, and
genuine scholars are known to have existed amongst them. By
the very nature of the case, moreover, it was rich parishes
which tended to attract the attention of appropriators, and

many vicars would accordingly have great and noble churches in which to take a pride. It is significant that today in the English countryside one often finds a large market town whose benefice is a vicarage, while all around are tiny villages which are rectories. The essential mark of the vicar was his personal residence. Many of the rectors too would be always resident, and not seldom poor; but others were well-connected men who had managed to obtain presentation to good unappropriated churches and were largely non-resident, leaving the parochial work to stipendiary chaplains who were removable at will and represent the tail-end of the clerical order in the medieval Church.

By the thirteenth century the English parochial system, which has been the main instrument for maintaining the Christian religion amongst us to this day, was complete. The other European countries too have all had similar systems, though it is in England that it survives in its classic form. In this form it is centred essentially on the benefice, which itself derives from Dark Ages feudalism. The idea of the parish, however, is much older, and can be traced back to the earliest Christian age. We shall conclude our survey of the origins of the English parish with a glance at pastoral developments which aimed at improving the work of the parish priest in his work amongst his people.

The Lateran Council of 1215 was followed in England by a spate of episcopal constitutions, which had various objects, prominent amongst them being the better instruction of the laity. This would require a more carefully educated clergy, and as a result many manuals, or *Summae,* of pastoral theology, were produced in England in the course of the thirteenth century. Two of the earliest of these, of about the same date as the Fourth Lateran Council, were a penitential written by Robert of Flamborough at the prompting of Bishop Richard Poore, and a *Summa* including pastoral as well as penitential matter, by Thomas of Chabham, subdean of Salisbury cathedral from 1206 to 1228 and vicar of Sturminster

Marshall, Dorset, throughout most of the same period. Greater discipline was now being required of the laity, the Lateran Council especially enjoining on everyone annual confession to the parish priest and communion at Easter. But if more regular use was from henceforth to be made of the confessional by the parishioner, his priest must be better skilled in the technique of hearing confessions and assigning penances. From this time penitentials become prominent in the corpus of religious literature. In a set of constitutions for his parochial clergy Alexander of Stavensby, Bishop of Lichfield 1224–37, included, amongst other material, a section on how to listen to and examine penitents. Other great bishops of the thirteenth century, such as Walter Cantilupe of Hereford and Grosseteste of Lincoln, were likewise concerned to make their clergy as authoritative and helpful as possible, not only as confessors but in their whole teaching ministry. Various treatises written by episcopal authority during this century for their parish priests deal with the proper expounding of such topics as the Ten Commandments, the vices and virtues, and the sacraments. Thus the office of parish priest is beginning to take on a distinctly "professional" look. In that it was helped by the tendency of the age to sharper definition and the schematization of knowledge. This was the period of the universities, with their elaborate curricula, their degrees, and such like. Not many, indeed, of the parochial clergy were as yet men trained in the schools, and Archbishop Pecham in his legislation issuing from the Provincial Council of Lambeth in 1281 made specific reference to the "ignorance of priests". But the parochial clergy, with all their deficiences, were the only material he or any other reforming prelate had to hand for the work of instructing Christ's people. Parish priests were now enjoined to expound four times a year the main articles of the Christian faith to their flocks.

In their synodal constitutions the thirteenth-century bishops tried to map out courses of instruction for the priests to pass on to their flocks, and to improve their efficiency as confessors. In a more formal way the bishops also wrote or commissioned tracts on the duties of the parish priest's office, circulating these at large through their dioceses. By the end of the century such tracts had become a more usual means of informing the parish priest than the synodal constitutions which had been particularly numerous in the half-century following the 1215 Lateran Council.

These tracts, not in themselves very well known even by professed medievalists today, were the forerunners of a series of manuals for parish priests in the fourteenth century. The best known of such manuals is John Mirk's *Instructions for Parish Priests,* composed in English verse at the very end of the century. But in many ways the most interesting is the *Oculus Sacerdotis,* usually listed first in the series.

The *Oculus Sacerdotis* appears to have been a work widely read and used by parish clergy of the fourteenth century and later, and some fifty manuscripts of it survive in England, though it has never been printed. Not the least interesting thing about the *Oculus* is that throughout the fourteenth century its authorship was generally unknown and the work accepted purely on its merits. Its author is now agreed to have been William of Pagula, who became vicar of Winkfield, Berkshire (then in the Salisbury diocese) in 1314. He was presented to this living by the dean and chapter of Salisbury. A man of the schools, a learned canonist and theologian, he may well have been a product of the scholarly circle which then flourished in Salisbury close. The year of his institution to Winkfield was the last year of the episcopate of Simon of Ghent, a prelate who made it a point of honour to encourage the cause of learning. It is somewhat remarkable to find a scholar like William of Pagula accepting a type of living, a vicarage, which would exclude him from any serious thoughts of non-residence. The distinguishing mark, in practice, of a vicar was not his low income compared with that of a rector, but his obligation to reside on his benefice in person. During the episcopate of Simon of Ghent 343 licences were granted in Salisbury diocese for non-residence, but of these only two were in favour of vicars, both of these to visit Rome for the

great Jubilee of 1300. William of Pagula was to remain vicar
of Winkfield for eighteen years, and there is no reason for
believing otherwise than that he was generally resident throughout that time. In 1322 he was penitentiary for the Reading
deanery, and later for the archdeaconry of Berkshire.

The *Oculus Sacerdotis* deals with the problems of the
parish priest in his confessional and as a teacher of faith and
morals. It does not, however, envisage him only as hearer
of confessions, or only as a preacher, but as one invested with
a solemn trust, the cure of souls in the widest sense. The pastor
lives amongst his people and is called to lead them and show
them the way to heaven. The *Oculus* is a work inspired above
all, as later medieval writers would put it, by a "zeal for
souls".

The book is in three parts, one of which, dealing with
sacramental confession, leans a good deal on the *Summa*
written a century before by Thomas of Chabham, also a priest
in the Salisbury diocese. The confessor, in questioning his
penitent, will have a care for such as do not "know the power
of wine", for those much given to fits of anger, and he will
be ready with helpful advice to expectant mothers. In Part II
the author sees the parish priest as teacher not only of the
great Christian doctrines but of simple daily duties. Parents
should be given advice on the care of their infant children.
Parishioners will be reminded not only of the obligation to
confess annually and communicate at Easter, but of the danger
of resorting to the black arts. Let the church and its graveyard
be treated with reverence. Four times a year the priest will
expound the articles of faith, the sacraments, the commandments, the vices and virtues, the works of mercy. Avarice
comes in for special denunciation, whether it be that of the
fraudulent executor, or of the merchant supplying short
measure, or of the archdeacon or rural dean demanding ex-
cessive fees for institutions to benefices. Part III treats of
the seven sacraments, especially the mass and holy matrimony.
Marriage is honourable, instituted by God himself. It has its
snares, however, warns William of Pagula. It is difficult to be

both a student and a married man. A dog or a horse is normally tried out before a man acquires it, but not so a wife. Once a man takes a wife he must put up with her.

The *Oculus* was not William's only work. While at Winkfield he also produced the *Summa Summarum*, a large compendium of practical canon law. His still vaster *Speculum Praelatorum* survives today in a single manuscript, in the library of Merton College. It contains sets of sermon *themata* for every Sunday and feast of the Christian year. William also wrote for the benefit of monks, and his *Speculum Religiosorum* survives in several manuscripts.

William's view of the cure of souls, as set forth in the *Oculus,* is all-embracing, and clearly envisages a parish priest knowing his people at first hand and settled amongst them over an extended period. A priest once appointed to a parish will regard the care of its people as his life's work. He will be interested both in their spiritual and their material concerns. It was in fact towards the close of his own fairly lengthy incumbency at Winkfield that William felt it his duty to take up his pen on behalf of his parishioners. It would appear that they were in some trouble at the time from the commissioners of the young Edward III demanding their services for cutting and carting wood in Windsor forest. In his *Epistola ad Regem Edwardum* their vicar made a bold protest against this abuse of the prerogative of purveyance. What William's parishioners actually thought of him we can never know; the sheer volume of his writings suggests that he spent far more time in his study than in his parish. Doubtless he had a curate. But his influence on other parish priests, over many years, must have been considerable. His *Oculus* is a reminder of the importance of the cure of souls in the maintenance of Christianity in the world. It was the classic parochial system, centred on the benefice with its assurance of security and personal responsibility, which made the pastoral office as envisaged by such men as William of Pagula possible.

St Luke in the second chapter of the Acts of the Apostles writes of the first Christians that they continued steadfastly in the teaching of the apostles, in fellowship, and in the breaking of bread and in prayers. From the very beginning the gathering together of believers, based on the Eucharist, has thus been at the heart of the Church's life. It is not the view of the present author that the idea of the *paroikia* is anything other than native to the Christian religion itself—an idea which presupposes a community of care and interest, under divinely commissioned leadership, looking forward as sojourners to the perfect society and worship of heaven.

Bibliography

For the development of the parochial system abroad, two essential books are: Catherine E. Boyd, *Tithes and Parishes in Medieval Italy* (New York, 1952); and Henry G. F. Beck, *The Pastoral Care of Souls in South-East France during the sixth Century* (Romae apud Aedes Universitatis Gregorianae, 1950). Imbart de la Tour, *Les Paroisses Rurales du IVe au XIe Siècle* (Paris, 1900), is a classic.

The subject of episcopal *familiae* may be studied in the following papers: Margaret Deanesly, "The Familia at Christchurch, Canterbury, 597–832" (*Essays in Medieval History* presented to T. F. Tout, Manchester, 1925); J. Armitage Robinson, "St Oswald and the Church of Worcester" (*British Academy Supplementary Papers, V*); and R. A. L. Smith, "The Early Community of St Andrew of Rochester, 604–c.1080" (*English Historical Review, CCXXXVIII*, September, 1945, pp. 289–99).

Parochial development on the Continent and in England is traced by G. W. O. Addleshaw, with particular reference to canon law, in three pamphlets published by the Borthwick Institute of Historical Research, York: *The Beginnings of the Parochial System* (n.d.); *The Development of the Parochial System from Charlemagne (768–814) to Urban II (1088–1099)* (1954); and *Rectors, Vicars, and Patrons in Twelfth and Early Thirteenth Century Canon Law* (1956). These pamphlets contain full bibliographies. Also valuable is D. Knowles, *The Monastic Order in England* (Cambridge, 1950) pp. 562-8, 595–600.

For early minsters: Margaret Deanesly, "Early English and Gallic Minsters" (*Transactions of the Royal Historical Society,* 4th series, XXIII, 1941); and for the buildings and lay-out of a seventh-century *monasterium,* Sir Charles Peers and C. A.

Ralegh Radford, "The Saxon Monastery of Whitby" (*Archaeologia*, LXXXIX, 1943, pp. 29-33). On the proprietary church, an important essay by Ulrich Stutz should be read, "The Proprietary Church as an element of Medieval Germanic Ecclesiastical Law", in *Medieval Germany, 911-1250. Essays by German Historians, II* (trans. G. Barraclough, Blackwell, 1948). The feudal background can be studied in F. L. Ganshof, *Qu'est-ce que la Féodalité?* (Eng. tr. P. Grierson, London, 1952).

For the late Saxon and early Norman periods: Gordon Ward, "The List of Saxon Churches in the Textus Roffensis" (*Archaeologia Cantiana*, XLIV, 1932); Gordon Ward, "The Lists of Saxon Churches in the Domesday Monachorum and White Book of St Augustine" (*Archaeologia Cantiana*, XLV, 1933); David C. Douglas, *The Domesday Monachorum of Christchurch Canterbury* (London, 1944). The article by William Page, "Some Remarks on the Churches of the Domesday Survey" (*Archaeologia*, 2nd series, XVI, 1915), remains indispensable, but must now be supplemented by the following works: H. C. Darby, *The Domesday Geography of Eastern England* (Cambridge, 1952); H. C. Darby and E. M. J. Campbell, *The Domesday Geography of South-East England* (Cambridge, 1962); H. C. Darby and I. S. Maxwell, *The Domesday Geography of Northern England* (Cambridge, 1962); H. C. Darby and R. Welldon Finn, *The Domesday Geography of South-West England* (Cambridge, 1967). All of these have sections on the churches. There is a valuable chapter on village churches in Reginald Lennard, *Rural England, 1086-1135* (Oxford, 1959); and urban churches are discussed with reference to one particular town by J. W. F. Hill, *Medieval Lincoln* (Cambridge, 1948).

The well-known book on the ordination of vicarages is R. A. R. Hartridge's *A History of Vicarages in the Middle Ages* (Cambridge, 1930), though this should be read in conjunction with two more recent works: D. Knowles, *The Religious Orders in England, II* (Cambridge, 1955), pp. 288-94; and H. Mayr-Harting, *The Acta of the Bishops of Chichester, 1075-1207* (Canterbury and York Society, 1964), pp. 57-62, with relevant documents. On William of Pagula see L. E. Boyle, "The Oculus

Sacerdotis and some other works of William of Pagula" (Transactions of the Royal Historical Society, 5th series, V, 1955); and W. A. Pantin, *The English Church in the Fourteenth Century* (Cambridge, 1955). For prebendal churches, reference may be made to A. Hamilton Thompson, *The English Clergy* (Oxford, 1947), pp. 105-7; and C. T. Flower and M. C. B. Dawes, *Registrum Simonis de Gandavo: Diocesis Saresbiriensis, 1297-1315* (Canterbury and York Society, 1934), pp xlvii-li.

The most complete collection of Anglo-Saxon charters is in W. de Gray Birch, *Cartularium Saxonicum* (3 vols., London, 1855-93). A. J. Robertson, *Anglo-Saxon Charters* (Cambridge, 1956), is useful for such documents as Alfred's bequest to Shaftesbury abbey and the list of the endowments of the minster of Lambourn. On the subject of the Conversion, Bede's *Historia Ecclesiastica,* of which there are several editions and translations (the latest by B. Colgrave, forthcoming), is the fundamental authority.

The whole field of Anglo-Saxon Christianity is surveyed by John Godfrey, *The Church in Anglo-Saxon England* (Cambridge, 1962). There is a valuable collection of Anglo-Saxon sources in *English Historical Documents, c.500-1042,* ed. Dorathy Whitelock (London, 1955). The latest attempt to compile a complete list of churches containing surviving Anglo-Saxon fabrics is by H. M. Taylor and Joan Taylor, *Anglo-Saxon Architecture* (2 vols., Cambridge, 1965). For San Clemente, the type of church which would be in the minds of returning Anglo-Saxon pilgrims from Rome, see L. E. Boyle, *A Short Guide to St Clement's* (Rome, 1963); and the beautifully produced *Roma, San Clemente,* by Carla Faldi Guglielmi, in the "Treasures of Christian Art" series. The transition from paganism to Christianity is studied by William A. Chaney in two interesting papers: "Paganism to Christianity in Anglo-Saxon England" (*Harvard Theological Review, LIII,* no 3, 1960); "Anglo-Saxon Church Dues: a Study in Historical Continuity" (*Church History, XXXII,* no. 3, 1963). For pastoral beginnings in the early Church, particularly with regard to the office of bishop, see S. L. Greenslade, "The Unit of Pastoral Care in the Early Church" (*Studies in Church History,* II, 1965, pp. 102-18).

Index